HOLD ON TO
HOPE

From Bipolar and Brokenness
to Healing and Wholeness

NICHOLE MARBACH

HOLD ON TO HOPE

I was thoroughly blessed reading *Hold On to Hope*. Knowing Nichole now, it's hard to believe that she was ever the disturbed woman portrayed in this book. The Lord enabled her to present her story in such a way that you will really feel what she went through. And when you read of how the truth set her free, you'll rejoice with her.

This book is for anyone who has dealt with rejection, self-hatred, drug or alcohol abuse, mental or emotional disorders, or anyone who doesn't know who they are in Christ. If the revelation of our new identity in Christ can set Nichole free, it will work for anyone. She is a trophy of God's grace.

Andrew Wommack
Founder, Andrew Wommack Ministries and Charis Bible College

From the minute I started reading Nichole's book, I did not want to put it down. Her story left me stunned. I couldn't believe what I was reading and the hell Nichole lived through growing up. Then, after living through Nichole's pain with her, I came to the most exciting part—the part of her story where Nichole was struck with the realization that she had been believing a whole bunch of lies for a whole bunch of years, and the dramatic trans-formation that took place when she began to believe the truth about God, herself, and her identity in Christ! I bet the devil is sorry he ever messed with Nichole Marbach!

I'm convinced that God's grace will cause her story to travel far and wide, setting people free all across this planet. After all, it was for freedom that Christ set us free! (Galatians 5:1)

Sandra McCollom
Founder, Freedom Living Ministries and author of I Tried Until I Almost Died

Nichole and I have traveled the world together, sharing the extravagant grace of Jesus Christ and the love of our good, good Daddy. We've experienced all sorts of situations together—times of exuberant joy and times where our faith was tested. After sharing so many plane rides, conferences, meals, and heart-to-hearts about life, Jesus, and relationships, I thought I knew her story…but this book has left me speechless.

Knowing the beautiful, joyful, shining light that Nichole is today and reading the details of her journey to healing, I am stunned by the compassion of Jesus and overwhelmed with the goodness of our Father. Nichole beautifully expresses how knowing our identity in Christ as God's dearly loved children is the key to our freedom from any bondage. I am so grateful that she's given us this record of her redemption so that hope will be restored to the hurting who may have given up. There is no one beyond the grip of God's grace.

Tricia Gunn
Founder, Parresia and author of Unveiling Jesus

DEDICATION

I would like to dedicate this book to my heavenly Father, who is the most amazing and loving Father anyone could want. He is truly the Daddy I always dreamed of having, and He's helping me live out all of my dreams. I love life because of Him!

Thank You, Daddy, for Your amazing and life-transforming love. Thank You for setting me free! May the world come to know just how good You are.

TABLE OF CONTENTS

ADDENDUM

PHOTOGRAPHS AND RESOURCES

ACKNOWLEDGMENTS

I would like to thank my husband, Claude, who stood by me in my darkest hour. He's the most awesome husband and father, and I am so blessed to have been married to him for over twenty-five years.

I also want to thank Renée Gray-Wilburn for doing such a phenomenal job editing this book and making my story come alive. The telling of my story wouldn't have been the same without Renée's amazing editing skills. I truly believe she was hand-picked by the Father for this project.

Thank you to Stephen Bransford for believing in my story from the moment he heard it. Stephen was responsible for my testimony becoming a part of Andrew Wommack's *Healing Journey* series on the *Gospel Truth* television program and website. Because of this, many have learned that they too can be free and whole because of Jesus. I'd also like to thank Stephen for his input and feedback throughout the writing process, which has allowed my story to impact even more people.

Thank you, too, to Andrew Wommack, whom I consider a spiritual father, for his teachings, his heart, and his wisdom that continually helps me walk out my healing. Being immersed in the Word of God through Andrew's teachings is a joy and adventure

I enjoy every day. Thank you, Andrew, for believing in my story and for your encouragement of how it will help many to witness the goodness of God.

Also, I'd like to offer a heartfelt thank-you to Joseph Prince for introducing me to God's grace. His book, *Destined to Reign*, was an absolute life-changer for me. I have grown immensely in the knowledge of Jesus and His finished work through Pastor Prince's teachings. Thank you for showing me that God is a good Daddy who is not mad at me but rather is madly in love with me!

Finally, I'd like to thank Joan Hunter of Joan Hunter Ministries for helping my heart receive God's healing. Joan's resources have equipped me to learn how to effectively minister to sick and hurting people. She is a blessing to me, the body of Christ, and all those who know her as a friend and mentor. Thank you, Joan, for being the "real deal" and for devoting your life to seeing people walk in the healing and wholeness that Jesus has provided.

"There is no pit so deep, that God's love is not deeper still."

– Corrie Ten Boom

"So if the Son liberates you [makes you free men], then you are really and unquestionably free."

(John 8:36, *Amplified Bible, Classic Edition*)

INTRODUCTION

"Nichole! Nichole! What are you doing?" I barely heard the frantic voice of my husband, Claude, as he swung our bedroom door open. I'm sure he was terrified with what he would find on the other side of that door. Would his wife be alive, or had she finally done the unthinkable?

Claude had good reason to be afraid. As he raced into our room, I stared at him dazed, completely covered in blood. My face, hands, and clothes were all a bloodied mess. Even my phone lying on the bed was spattered with the liquid of life that once coursed through my veins. The sound of my husband's frightened voice is the only thing that stopped me in the middle of slitting my wrist with a razor blade, on the verge of blacking out, not caring if I lived or died.

Earlier that day, I had finally given in to the voices in my head telling me that life wasn't worth living. I had come so far. I had been sober for a full year and a half after realizing I had a drinking problem. But, for some reason, that day I listened to the voices again. They convinced me that the only way I would get through the pain of life was to escape with alcohol.

Obediently, I headed off to the liquor store to purchase a bottle of wine, making sure there was no one I knew who would catch me red handed. I had heard the gossip: I was the "unstable, bipolar, alcoholic crazy woman" in the neighborhood. I didn't want to risk fueling that gossip and embarrassing myself or my kids.

I paced the store, fighting the temptation, but it proved to be too strong, and I gave in. My kids were in school, so I only had a small window of opportunity to numb my pain in a short amount of time. I had to be present when they came home.

In my kitchen, I started playing the *Abba Gold* album very loudly to give me the courage to follow through with my plan and to hopefully drown out the tormenting voices. I was scared of myself and how each relapse brought me into a darker place. I never knew how my story would end. I never knew what I would do under the influence of alcohol. Would I go too far?

I had once researched to see if Christians who commit suicide go to heaven, but I wasn't sure of the answer. I didn't want to go to hell, but I also didn't want to continue living in hell on earth. I was tormented and willing to take the chance either way.

I took the bottle from the bag and decided I would just open it and smell it but not drink it. I tried convincing myself that I wouldn't follow through to the end, but I knew I was lying. I was supposed to call my Alcoholics Anonymous sponsor at times like this, but I rationalized, "Why bother anymore? It doesn't do any good, and I can't handle this pain any longer." But I also remembered how great I felt earning that one-year sobriety coin from AA and how long it took me to get it. Before that, I had received a one-month or three-month coin, only to go back the following week admitting that I had relapsed yet again, and then the coin would mean nothing.

After removing the cork and smelling it several times, I succumbed to the haunting voices telling me, "You can do it and not tell anyone. Just go ahead and do it. The pain will be gone. Go ahead and do it." After taking the first sip, I had a thought that I believe every recovering alcoholic or addict has after the first sip: *You took a sip and relapsed, you might as well drink the whole bottle now.*

I had barely had anything to eat that day because it was one of those days of tormented thinking that had been brewing for a couple of weeks. I could barely function, let alone eat. I couldn't do anything to escape the torment, or at least that's what I had thought. Bipolar disorder, which I had been diagnosed with, was considered incurable. I figured I'd have to just suck it up and live with the mental torment for the rest of my life.

After that first sip, I quickly downed a couple of glasses. I then decided to do what I typically did whenever I relapsed on alcohol. I took out a razor blade, which I carried everywhere I went, and started cutting my wrist. As the razor cut through layer upon layer of skin, I felt immediate and extreme physical pain, yet no more emotional pain. What a relief I had experienced in that moment!

Within seconds, splatters of blood were all over my kitchen counter. I knew my kids would be home soon, and I definitely didn't want them to see me in this condition. I sheltered them from my bipolar episodes whenever possible. I wanted them to have a better life than I did. After drinking the wine and cutting my wrist, I did something that I never thought I'd do: I called my neighbor.

Melissa knew things weren't right with me. I called her and told her what was going on because I couldn't live with the guilt of hiding it. There was a part of me that wanted help, and I knew I'd get it if I shared my tormenting adventures with others. But there was another part of me that wanted to hide it so I could continue to escape from the pain, or even end my life.

Melissa hurried into my kitchen and immediately saw the blood all over me and my counter. "Go upstairs to your bedroom," she instructed me. "I'll clean up down here and watch the kids until Claude gets home."

By the time Melissa got to my house, I had finished the entire bottle of wine—on an empty stomach. I was officially drunk. I somehow stumbled to my bedroom and got into bed. It was not long afterward when I heard a voice tell me to get another razor from under my bathroom counter. I took the razor out of the package and knew I needed to rip the plastic handle off so I could continue cutting myself with a new blade. I used my hands instead of a tool to do so.

I cut my fingers as I desperately tried to remove the handle, but I didn't care. My only focus was to continue numbing the emotional pain and the shame and guilt from what I had just done. Blood was everywhere, but I didn't care about that either. I knew I had once again disappointed my husband and my supportive friends. I knew they were losing faith in me and starting to give up because they were at their wits' end with how to help me. I had already given up on myself.

Finally, thankfully, the handle came off, and I fell back into bed. I took the razor and continued to slit my wrist deeper and deeper, watching the blood flow as I began blacking out. Apparently, I had called my friend Ingrid during this episode and said, "Now you can reject me. I messed up again. You can reject me now because I know you will ultimately reject me."

Ingrid was a continual support and encouragement to me during my bipolar adventure. She reassured me that she wasn't going anywhere, but I never really believed it in my heart. I hung up the phone and continued to slit my wrist. Alcohol and self-injury are a very dangerous and potentially lethal combination. I knew it, and everyone else around me knew it. My family and friends never knew when I would have another bipolar destructive manic episode. They were sometimes afraid to leave me alone, with good reason. I was even afraid to be alone with myself for fear of taking my own life.

I heard Claude open the door and desperately yell my name, jolting me back to reality and causing me to cease from cutting myself any longer. This is a scene from our lives we will never forget. Claude, scared and helpless, watched as the wife he deeply loved sat covered in blood, after attempting suicide yet again—so drunk she wasn't even present. He could not fix her. He could not rescue her.

How did I get here? What went so horribly wrong? How did I become so hopeless?

PART I

TRAUMA

CHAPTER 1

SHATTERED TRUST

"You've been awarded legal guardianship," the judge pronounced to my father, John. During the meeting to determine who would be awarded custody of me and my younger sister, Wendy, my mother, Linda, had slipped John a note, which read: "You can have the house and the kids, but I would like the car." My mother had been having an affair with a man who didn't like children. She knew that she'd have to give up her kids in order to keep this man in her life. So, my mom abandoned and rejected her own children in order to try to fill the void of love. Abandonment would be a theme throughout my entire childhood, and it was a painful price to pay due to unhealthy and emotionally unavailable parents.

Linda was raised in foster homes, which was traumatic for her. She was molested in some of the homes, and as a result, she grew up with a lot of unhealed wounds that affected her behavior. When Linda discovered that she was pregnant out of wedlock with my first sister, Karen, my grandmother (who was granted custody of her children again at one point), sent her to a home for unwed mothers. My grandmother influenced my mother to give Karen up for adoption.

Then, just a couple of years later, Linda found herself pregnant again by Karen's dad, Kyle, and gave birth to my older sister,

Sheryl. By now, Linda and Kyle had married, even though Kyle was an abusive boyfriend. Marriage did not end his abuse, as Kyle continued to physically attack both my mom and Sheryl. Linda eventually divorced Kyle and became a single mother. But, for some reason, when Sheryl was about ten, Linda sent her to live with her abusive dad and stepmom.

My Father

John was born when his mother was about forty years old. He was called an "accident," as his brother and sister were about sixteen and seventeen years older than he was. I never met my paternal grandfather, but I was told that both he and my grandmother were alcoholics. I had experienced my grandmother's alcoholism whenever we kids would stay at her house on the weekends so that my dad could go out and party. In fact, the first thing we did when we went to her house was to go to the store and get her a stash of beer. Often, at family parties, all of my relatives would drink heavily, and I'd hear my grandma slur her words.

My dad rarely talked about his childhood, but I know he endured pain that he had been suppressing his whole life. He had many unhealed wounds and addictions he never dealt with. When my mom and dad first met, they went out on a couple of dates, but my dad wanted to break up with my mom. But my mom had become pregnant with me, and they decided that getting married was the right thing to do. The result is that I was born to two people who didn't love each other. My parents, John and Linda, did get married eventually, but they had a loveless marriage, which affected me and my sister Wendy, who was born a couple of years later.

Children need parents they can trust and depend on, and they need to feel safe, loved, and protected. My dad didn't know how to love me, and I received very inconsistent love from him. As a result, at a young age, I didn't feel safe and told myself that I couldn't trust anyone, even my own parents. One of my life's subconscious missions became trying to win "unavailable love" from my father, as well as others. I thought that if I could win this love, it would prove once and for all that I was worthy of love.

One moment my dad was playing catch with me, and the next moment he was touching me inappropriately. One moment he would make me laugh, and the next moment he looked like he wanted to murder me. His look of disgust brought such fear to my little soul, I'd tremble. I experienced extreme terror from my father because he used fear as a tactic to get us to obey. I'd often hear him spanking Sheryl with his belt, and it frightened me. Thankfully, he never did this to me, but I couldn't help but think when I did something wrong, *Am I next?*

This inconsistent behavior was very confusing for me as a child. It caused me to grow up with the mindset of always fearing getting in trouble, which I unknowingly carried into my adult years. A child cannot trust a parent who terrorizes her. And a child cannot trust a parent who is supposed to be protecting her but instead touches her inappropriately.

Even as a toddler, my days were filled with chaos and turmoil. They were filled with fighting parents who loved to have people over to play cards until the middle of the night, doing drugs and drinking alcohol in the same room where I played. Later, as an adult, I found the picture below of myself as a toddler, holding a beer can. I was told that I'd drink the leftover beer from the cans that were lying around. Everyone laughed at me, thinking it was funny. But I don't think it's funny to give alcohol to toddlers.

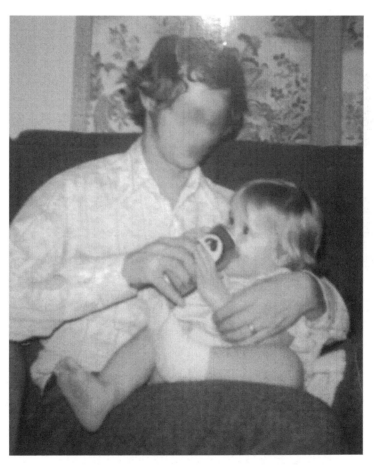

My Father Helping Me Drink Beer

Me as a Toddler with a Leftover Beer

I'm convinced that my exposure to alcohol at this young age profoundly affected me. I recall nights when I was so tired I'd fall asleep under my mom's chair while everyone partied. No one seemed to care that young children were in the same room while they drank and did drugs.

My father's addiction to drugs and alcohol terrified me. Because of his addictions, I still have horrific memories of anything related to drugs or alcohol. In fact, even now, the smell of marijuana brings back a flood of negative memories. I think about how the enemy (Satan) used drugs to try to destroy my life through my father. I used to watch smoke swirl above my dad's head and witness him morph into a completely different person whom I didn't like one bit. I also remember my sister and I rolling Dad's joints in the morning. He would be dressed in a suit and tie, ready to drive us to school before he went to work, and Wendy and I took turns pressing down the handle of the roller, momentarily forgetting our pain.

A tray of marijuana was kept on top of our refrigerator until I was about ten, when my mom called to tell my dad that we didn't want to see it anymore. We constantly complained to her how embarrassing it was for us to see it up there and have to pretend that it didn't exist and never talk about it. A mother of one of Wendy's friend's once called my mom to tell her that her daughter wouldn't be allowed at our house anymore if the marijuana continued to stay out. We were ashamed to have friends over because of the drugs on the fridge, proudly displayed for all to see. But we were scared to tell Dad how we felt; we knew we'd be in trouble for expressing our feelings.

Growing up, I never knew when my dad would be under the influence of alcohol or drugs. My trust was shattered, and I grew up learning to examine his every move. I never knew what mood I would find him in. I was so afraid of making him upset that I couldn't be myself. I quickly learned to walk on eggshells during my childhood and teen years. I didn't know how to use my voice but instead just pleased others in order to survive. I found that when we have to constantly analyze the actions of others, with chaos all around, there is no peace.

Anxiety became my most natural feeling—more familiar to me than peace, and this carried into my adult life. There are times even now when something will happen–even something minor—and I have to remind myself that I'm safe now, and it's not the end of the world. The inconsistent, unavailable love that I continually endured was literally a "crazy maker" in my life and made my childhood a living hell. Yet, I stuffed everything inside, never learning how to cope with pain.

My Mother

Like my father, my mother didn't have real parenting growing up. She was abandoned by her father, who died of cirrhosis of the liver. Being sexually abused and taken away from her home took a toll on her. Unfortunately, even though I have some great memories of my mom, like my dad, she was never emotionally available for us kids. In many ways, my mom always acted like a child her whole life. As I grew up, I became her mother and took care of her. After she divorced my dad, and then my stepfather, Richard, I ended up taking care of the house the way a husband would. I did all of the yard work and whatever else needed to be done after a full day of school and track practice.

Linda married and divorced a total of four times and went down some rough roads in her life. She never dealt with the pain of her past, which only served to create scenarios for more pain. As a child and a teen, I'd hear my mother crying out to Jesus, saying, "Jesus, I don't want to live anymore. Come and take me home." As a little girl, this is devastating. It caused me to live in fear that my mom would someday leave me or take her own life. I think I even believed that Jesus would take her home and answer her prayer. I never talked to my mom about it but rather continued to push the pain down deep inside. By hearing how my mom wanted to die, it caused me to be extra careful when I talked to her. It made me want to take care of her and rescue her. I managed the house for her so she wouldn't be burdened.

The inconsistent love and care I received from both of my parents only served to increase the trauma I carried as a little girl. The only bond I formed was with animals, and even that was shattered. I remember when my girlfriends in high school decided to throw me a surprise sixteenth birthday party. My mom knew about it, and she also knew that one of the gifts they were giving me was a puppy. I'll never forget seeing Alex in the box! I was so excited to have a dog for the first time. I loved that dog and tried to train him to the best of my ability, but I didn't know how. He didn't listen to me, but I loved him anyway.

I continued to go back and forth to my dad's house, and when I did, my mom was responsible for Alex. One day, Alex ran away, and I was devastated. I looked everywhere for him. I called the local animal shelters, and one of them said they had him. Elated, I got my Alex back. I was determined to never let that happen again but to take better care of him.

Alex slept in my bed with me when I was home. Unfortunately, one day when I went to my mom's house, she told me Alex ran away again. My mom was planning on moving into an apartment, and I knew that I'd eventually have to find a home for him. I wanted the best home I could find, and one where I could still visit him. My plan was not for him to run away and never see him again. For days I looked everywhere in the neighborhood, calling his name. I called the animal shelters and went to see if he was there. He was lost, and my heart was shattered. I felt responsible.

It wasn't until a couple of months later I discovered that my mom, who was a waitress at the time, gave him away to one of her customers. She lied to me, which shattered my trust even more. When I found out, I asked her if she took the person's name and number so I could say goodbye to Alex, but she didn't. I had so much anger and rage about this. My friend who had kept Alex before he was given to me was also upset because she would've taken him back if she had known.

This was such a cruel thing that my mom did, and I had to forgive her for it. There was nothing else I could do, but it definitely broke whatever trust I had for her. She knew how much I loved that dog, and he was mine. It took me quite some time to get over the pain of my mother's betrayal.

With my trust shattered once again, I began to question my existence. I felt like a burden in so many ways. I began developing mindsets that continually shouted at me: "There must be something wrong with you"; "No one wants you because you're unlovable"; "Everyone will eventually reject you"; "You can't trust anyone."

When my parents divorced, I had to adjust to going back and forth to both parents' homes. It was difficult, but I dealt with it the best I could. One thing that helped me was excelling in athletics. I was very, very fast. I could beat all the boys in the neighborhood when we organized running and swimming races. I'm sure I humiliated many of them in front of their friends! Whatever sport I did, I did it well. I believe that participating in sports helped me cope with what was going on in my life. I was a fighter. I had perseverance. Those qualities have helped me endure whatever I've faced. Even stepparents.

CHAPTER 2

STEPPARENT PAIN

In addition to having two inconsistent parents, unhealthy stepparents also entered my life without me having a say. In a day, my world changed from pain to much more pain! I will never forget that day.

I was playing my Atari video game when my dad's new girlfriend came over the house to babysit me. She was much younger (about sixteen years younger) than he was, and I didn't like her from the start. Out of nowhere she asks, "How would you like it if I moved in with you guys?" I was devastated!

But it didn't matter what I thought, because like it or not, she was going to move in. I lied and acted excited because I didn't want to get in trouble. When she did move in, my life drastically changed for the worse. Even though my dad had unhealed wounds, I bonded with him more than I did my mom at the time. But when his girlfriend, Mary, moved in, he emotionally abandoned us. Mary became his entire world, and all he cared about was making her happy. From the moment she entered our lives, she controlled not only my dad but also me and my sister.

Mary was very young and never wanted to have kids. One of the first things she did was to put nearly all of our toys in the garage. She even threw out my favorite blanket, which I used for comfort. And, we were never allowed to make a mess because she was a neat freak. She vacuumed and made sure the house was totally spotless every day. We weren't allowed to have any toys lying out. She constantly monitored us. We were not free to be children.

Mary wanted my dad to save every penny so they could have nice vacations and buy things for themselves, yet we kids got practically nothing. I learned to hate Mary and despised going to my dad's house. I could never understand why he let her control his every move, including what he was allowed to eat. I used to think, *Why can't he stand up for himself, and why can't he stand up for us?*

Mary was very controlling about many things. She would make a certain meal on a particular night of the week—every week. When I went school shopping with her for clothes, I was only allowed to pick out minimal outfits, and they had to be cheap. She picked out our "Tuesday, Thursday" outfits that we were required to wear every Tuesday and Thursday so that they'd end up at her house and not my mom's.

Being a light sleeper, she liked to go to bed early. Because of this, we had to go to bed early as well. We were never allowed to stay up late to watch TV or go downstairs to get a drink of water during the night. I'd wet my bed in the middle of the night rather than take a chance on waking her up.

I got to the point that I wanted to stay at my mom's house instead of my dad's. When 6:30 P.M. came, and I knew my dad and Mary would show up at my mom's to bring us to their house because of the custody agreement, I'd start hugging my mom, telling her

I didn't want to leave. But I had no choice. I'd cry, dreading the car ride to my dad's, feeling like I was being taken to prison. But I could never tell my dad how I felt, or I'd get in big trouble.

As we became teenagers, my sister and I decided it was better to sleep at friends' houses when it was the weekend that we were supposed to be at our dad's. There were times when we lied and stayed at our mom's house, just because we didn't want to go to Dad's. We hated it there. Our house was no longer our home; it was a jail cell! We were never even given a key to our own house.

Teenage Trauma

Once when I was about sixteen, I realized that I forgot a shirt at my dad's house that I wanted to wear. I knew Mary would be home, but I wasn't sure if my dad would be at home or work. I was so afraid that I'd find them high from marijuana. I must have wanted to wear that shirt very badly to risk going over to my dad's unannounced!

After Wendy's friend's mother called my mom to tell my dad about the pot, he stopped doing drugs in front of us or when we were home, which was a relief. However, I still risked him being high whenever I had to call him on a day that we weren't going to his house, or in this instance, going there unexpectedly. I walked to the front door and saw that the storm door was open, revealing the screen door, which let me know someone was home. I listened at the door for a minute to make sure it was okay to enter. I wanted to see if I could hear them doing drugs together. I didn't know what to do.

This was my own home, yet they never gave me a key, and it never felt like my home. I didn't know if I should walk in or knock. I decided to knock. Mary let me in and was upset that I didn't just walk in. Little did she know how her controlling behavior affected me.

She told my dad what had happened, and I'll never forget the next day when I went to his house. He stormed into my room, and in a rage, grabbed my face in his hands, squeezing it tightly enough to cause pain. He then threw me up against the wall and held me in that position with his hand holding my face so I couldn't move. He screamed at me, "Don't you ever knock on the door to your own home again!" He proceeded to tell me how hurt Mary was that I did that.

He could never see things from my perspective. He had no idea the hurt and pain we experienced that he caused by bringing Mary into our house so they could live together. He had no idea that his home did not feel like a home. I believe he felt guilt and shame and had to take it out on me. Some time later, he truly did feel guilty for the physical abuse he caused me, and he cried and apologized. I have learned that abusers will continue to abuse their victims then feel guilty. Then they apologize, making it seem genuine, in order to keep the cycle going.

This happened more than once, but I was still afraid to tell him how I felt. It wouldn't have done any good, as he never listened or did anything to help us, especially when it was related to Mary. I tried to keep what little peace I could by bottling everything inside. I went into survival mode.

Another traumatic teenage memory is from my sophomore year in high school. I was asked to the Homecoming dance and was excited to go with my date and all of my friends. I found out that Homecoming fell on my dad's weekend to have us kids. I was devastated. I knew that Mary always wanted to go to bed early, which is why my curfew was 10:00 P.M. at the latest on weekends. I begged my dad to be able to stay out late for this very special occasion, but the latest they would let me stay out was 10:30. All of my friends were able to stay out much later. It was embarrassing and humiliating.

The couple we drove with dropped me off at my dad's house and my date kissed me goodnight, upset that I had to go home so early. I never heard from him again. Why couldn't my dad stand up for me being able to stay out a little later on a special night?

My dad had promised us for years that he'd never marry his girlfriend. We had hoped that he'd eventually break up with her. This was my dad's third marriage, and he had told us he didn't want to get married or have another divorce.

But then the day came when he went back on his word. It was my dad's day of the week for us to go to his house, so he came to pick us up from my mom's at 6:30 sharp. Something was different that day. Mary wasn't with him. She was always with him 24/7, and we never saw him without her. We were excited at first, thinking we could finally have some alone time with our father.

During the car ride home, however, we quickly figured out the reason he was by himself. He told us in the car that he and Mary were getting married. Tears started streaming down my face. I tried to hide them for fear of getting in trouble. My sister was crying too. I know my dad knew we were crying as much as we tried to hide it, but ultimately everything was all about his happiness and not ours. This was a devastating blow to us. We knew that we would be stuck with Mary for the remainder of our days in that house. The only good part is that they got married in Las Vegas, so we didn't have to witness it.

Stepparent #2

Not only did I have to face the consequences of my dad marrying Mary, but my mother also decided to get married to Tony not long after she divorced my dad. I didn't like Tony, and he didn't like me—a fact he never tried to hide. Both of my stepparents favored Wendy over me. I was treated very differently from her, which made me feel abnormal and unlovable and only confirmed all the negative messages that had been written on my heart since I was abused. It was very difficult at my age to not feel tainted. It was hard to feel so rejected and abandoned and not do anything about it.

I'll never forget the day my mom and Tony married. Even though I hated him, I decided to make peace. As soon as they were married, I went to him, pulled on his blazer and excitedly said, "Hi, Dad!" I'll never forget how he looked at me with a completely straight face without saying a word. He ignored my attempt to love him and make peace with him. I was soon to learn this was only a foreshadowing of what was to come.

He picked on me for every mistake, and at times he was physically abusive. Sometimes I could no longer stand his constant harassment, and I'd yell that I hated him and wanted my dad. He didn't like that and would punish me with more physical abuse.

I wasn't the only one whom Tony abused, however. One night I heard him raping my mom. I was very protective of my mother during this time, and knowing that there was nothing I could do to help her was devastating. I remember her repeatedly yelling "No!" at him, then screaming, but he didn't care and continued to rape her with us in the house.

Tony always showed us two sides of himself: the church side, where he put on a smile for everyone and pretended to be a holy Christian and a perfect husband and stepfather; and then his real side, which was angry, self-righteous, and hypocritical.

We did go to church, which I thoroughly enjoyed. I felt different when I was there. I remember hearing people speaking in tongues, and I saw healing miracles right before my eyes. I was in awe of God and fell in love with the Lord. One day, my mom and Tony had me pray a salvation prayer to receive Jesus as my Savior. I wanted to receive Jesus; I wasn't forced to. While I was saying that prayer, I immediately started weeping. The Holy Spirit touched me deeply, because it was very unlike me to become emotional and cry. I felt the Lord's presence at that moment, as He came to live in me and make me a new creation.

From this point on, I'd talk to God and read the Bible. One of Tony's friends gave me a children's Bible when we went to his house one day. I was so excited to get a gift, especially a Bible. When I was at my dad's house, I'd sometimes lie underneath my bed and read my Bible. I didn't understand all I was reading, but

I still enjoyed it. Even back then, God was preparing me for my calling and giving me a foundation in His Word.

I was so excited about God, that on several occasions, I tried to share the gospel with my dad because I didn't want him to go to hell. One memory I have is of my dad and his friend high on drugs as I tried to share a story about Jesus with them. They started laughing hysterically and making fun of me. I felt humiliated but also proud for having shared the truth with them.

Dangerous Legalism

Although I'm thankful for Tony and my mom praying with me for salvation, I came to understand how Tony's view of God also caused damage in my life. I remember how my mom cried out in pain on her bed one day with her door shut, and I wasn't allowed to see her. Tony believed that it was wrong to go to a doctor and refused to take my mom to the hospital, even though she was screaming in agony.

It was difficult for me to watch my mom in pain and not be able to do anything to help her. I wanted to rescue her but couldn't. Eventually, Tony took her to the hospital. We learned that she had a large cancerous tumor and had both ovarian and colon cancer. My church prayed for her healing before her surgery. Her doctor said that the tumor he removed from her was one of the largest he'd ever seen.

When she had surgery, we had to spend an entire week at my dad's house. I wanted to be with her and was worried that she'd die either during the surgery or afterward because of the cancer. I was afraid that if she died, I'd have to permanently live at my dad's "prison." We kids had nothing to do there, and we weren't allowed to do anything. I didn't want that, and I had no one to talk to about it.

I was also afraid because of some misconceptions I had about the end times. Growing up with my mom, I heard a lot about Jesus coming back and how some people would be left behind. I also learned about the antichrist coming in the end times, who would make everyone get the number "666" stamped on their forehead. I was taught that if you got that number stamped on you, you went to hell. I was terrified that if my mom died, I'd have to live with John, my atheist father, who would make me get 666 stamped on my forehead, and I'd spend eternity in hell because of it.

I was also afraid that if Jesus came He would take Linda, and I'd certainly be left behind because I wasn't good enough. As a result, I'd have to live with my dad. Fear and torment engulfed me.

In many ways, I felt just as unsafe in my stepdad's house as I did in my dad's house. Just like with Mary, I had no freedom to just be me. I had to watch my every move and walk on eggshells because of him. Also, Tony would go into my room and record classical music over my favorite rock music bands if they weren't Christian bands. I listened to a lot of Christian music, but I also liked some secular music. But I wasn't allowed to listen to anything secular in the house. He'd snoop through my music and tape over it. He was very legalistic, putting constant fear in me that if he was mad at me then God must be mad at me too. I naively believed that if Tony always went to church, he must have a right relationship with God.

My stepdad enjoyed hurting me and retaliating. My mother started favoring me because of how I was always being picked on, and Tony realized it. He knew that she had more love for me than for him, and he enjoyed taking that out on me. My mom eventually decided to divorce Tony, which I was thankful for, but I wasn't happy when she told me that I was the reason they got divorced. It just gave me one more opportunity to feel guilty and unworthy.

I lived with four emotionally unhealthy, immature adults with unhealed wounds throughout my childhood, which took a grave toll on me. It shattered my trust in people and caused me to live in a constant state of anxiety and fear of getting in trouble. I had absolutely no rest mentally or emotionally. I truly believed that I was nothing more than a burden and that everyone would be better off without me.

CHAPTER 3

THE PATH OF SELF-DESTRUCTION

"Ouch!" I yelled, reeling in pain. Somehow, I twisted my ankle on a huge rock playing Hide-and-Seek with a group of kids from the apartment complex where my mom and my sister and I lived. I'd spend hours playing in a field across from the apartments, using my imagination to take me into a different world. It was a world outside of reality, a fantasy world. A world with adventure and fun instead of pain, chaos, and turmoil. Today I was back in that field trying to escape. But the physical pain I had just encountered snapped me back to reality.

I looked down at my ankle, and the injury didn't look that bad, even though it hurt like crazy. I looked around, and no one was near me. I decided to see if any kids were nearby because I had an idea that might help me get some of the love and nurturing I so craved. I purposely banged my ankle against the rock over and over so the injury became bad enough to send me to the doctor.

My plan worked. Soon, the kids found me, and I was limping. Now, I truly was in pain! The physical pain that I endured as my ankle crashed against the rock with each blow was totally worth the attention and love I received from the injury. A couple of the kids helped walk me home. I had to go to my dad's house that night, and I couldn't wait to tell him what happened. After we got to his house and he saw my ankle, he told me that he didn't think it looked too bad and that I'd be fine. I was crushed!

At some point later that evening, I was in the bathroom when I suddenly had another idea. I was desperate to get what I really wanted: attention at home and at school. I made sure the door was locked and decided to bang my ankle over and over against the bathtub. I tried to be as quiet as possible as to not get into trouble. It hurt, but I was determined to continue the self-infliction. The end result would be worth it in my eyes. I left the bathroom in pain, limped around, and then returned to the bathroom for another round. By now, my ankle was completely bruised and swollen.

Once again, I showed it to my dad, and he was finally concerned enough to take me to the hospital to get it checked out. I never told anyone what I had done until years later when I met with counselors. The doctor determined that I had sprained my ankle, so he bandaged it and gave me crutches. For me, crutches were the ultimate attention-getter, which made me very satisfied with my plan.

When I returned home from the hospital, the pain was severe, and I had to go to bed. I woke up that night in excruciating pain, and part of me regretted my decision to hurt myself. I wanted to awaken my dad to give me pain medicine, but I was scared. Children who grow up in healthy homes would have no problem awaking their parents if there was a problem. This wasn't the case with me. I decided instead that I'd have to live with the pain because the thought of being terrorized by my father for waking him and my stepmom was much worse than my ankle hurting.

The Intrigue of Self-Injury

As a child and teen, I'd often bang my head against walls and punch myself. I pulled my hair, stabbed myself with safety pins, and picked freckles out. All this caused pain, but I was able to hide it so no one knew.

One day, I found a razor blade in the house. I pretended to start shaving my legs, being careful not to get caught. I rubbed the razor up and down my legs, not realizing how sharp a razor actually is and that if I pressed too hard I'd cut myself. I bled immediately. For some reason, this intrigued me. I felt pain, yet I couldn't stop. Curiously, I watched the blood run down my legs. I knew I had to stop because if I got caught, I'd pay for it.

As I have often reflected on that incident, it occurred to me that any healthy child who cut herself with a razor would stop immediately due to the pain. People are adverse to pain, especially children. But for me, the emotional pain far outweighed any physical pain I could cause myself.

I found that the only way for me to express the rage I was experiencing on the inside due to the verbal, physical, and sexual abuse I had endured was to hurt myself. I had no one to talk to whom I could trust. I had no role models of what healthy communication even looked like. My bottled-up anger and feelings of being defective, unwanted, and a burden to those around me left me not knowing how to cope with what was happening inside of me.

At the top of the list for why I hurt myself was the sexual abuse. By far, this took the biggest toll on me emotionally. Being touched inappropriately made me feel uncomfortable and violated. The little trust I had in people was shattered during these moments.

One of my abusers was a boy my age. One day, he and I, along with some kids from the apartment complex, were in that same field where I hurt my ankle. He told the others to stand guard and tell us if anyone was coming. I remember lying in the dirt with him on top of me, doing things I didn't want him to do. I felt uncomfortable and wanted him to stop, but he wouldn't.

He touched me in places that others had touched me inappropriately, bringing up horrific memories. I felt tainted and dirty. I froze. I wanted to run, but I was terrified at what he might do to me. When abuse occurred, I was always told, "you better not tell anyone." This kid was a bully, and I remember him punching me after this incident. I was afraid of him. All of those kids who were keeping watch knew what was taking place, yet none helped me, further disintegrating my trust in people.

My worst experience, which occurred years later, was being raped as a child. This incident of being drugged and raped deeply impacted my soul. Additionally, the verbal and physical abuse that I regularly encountered planted thoughts in my mind that I was a bad person whom no one wanted to love. I found any means possible to escape the pain. In addition to self-injury, I discovered another quicker, easier way to numb my feelings of unworthiness, self-hatred, insecurity, mistrust, and rage. I found alcohol.

Finding Alcohol

"Do you want to go to a party at Andrew's house?" my then-best friend asked me. I was a fifteen-year-old high school sophomore and was well acquainted with Andrew's reputation for wild parties. Rumor had it that alcohol was always available to underage drinkers. "Sure," I told my friend, well aware of what I was getting into.

"Can I spend the night at your house?" I asked my friend. In order to stay out late, I had to spend the night at a friend's house. My dad would always say yes to me staying with a friend because it gave him the opportunity to get high without worrying about us being there.

"I'll ask my mom," my friend replied, "but I'm sure you can stay over like you always do." I got ready for the party by using a curling iron and lots of hair spray to fix my hair in a typical 1980's style. Then we waited for a couple other girlfriends to come over so we could all go together.

When we arrived at the party I felt very awkward. I was happy that I was with my friends because my self-worth at the time was based on whom I knew. Not long after we got there, I drank my very first wine cooler, and it tasted so good. I drank another one after that, and then another. I'm not sure how many I ended up drinking that night. I had never had the opportunity to drink as much as I wanted before. Not being used to all that alcohol, I quickly became drunk.

I remember acting obnoxious and hearing people talk about me and point to me. I also remember feeling dizzy and lying on the floor at one point. This night became a turning point in my life, as I vowed to continue numbing my pain with alcohol. I remember feeling free with no anxiety. It felt great! I could forget the pain for a time. I believed that I needed to continue drinking in order to be okay. Alcohol became my new best friend.

After that party, many weekends were spent at my friend's house drinking. Oftentimes, I would vomit and have a hangover the following day, but that didn't stop me. I even put myself in danger at times with my friends in order to find someone old enough to buy us alcohol since we were underage.

One time, after cruising a well-known road where people picked each other up, my friends and I asked some guys in our car if they could buy alcohol for us. We went down a dark alley behind the store, and when they came back to give it to us, I suddenly became petrified, wondering if they were going to rape and murder us. We were in a not-so-nice neighborhood, with two much-older guys buying alcohol for us. Alcohol can cause people to do dangerous things, and this was one of many incidents where I feared for my life, simply because I wanted to drink to numb the pain.

In some ways, numbness outweighed the risks I encountered. Nothing worked better than alcohol. Sometimes, I'd even drive home drunk, swerving all over the road and praying that I'd make it home and not hurt anyone or get a DUI. I honestly don't know how I ever escaped getting pulled over by the police.

If I couldn't spend the night at a friend's house, I'd go to my mom's. If she was already asleep, I'd sleep in my car. Anything so I didn't have to go my dad's house. The pain that I experienced in those moments was overwhelming. I felt as though I didn't belong anywhere, then I felt guilty for hiding my drinking because I never once got caught.

My mom was quite naïve. I could never do anything wrong in her eyes because I took care of her and was a "good girl." She had no idea that I was having sex with my boyfriend and getting drunk all the time. I learned to hide my drinking really well.

One time, I thought for sure she'd figure it out and I'd end up disappointing her and getting in trouble. I had gone to an apartment with my boyfriend and another couple, and we drank a lot. I was the one, however, who drank the most and got the drunkest. I spent the entire night vomiting, and when we finally had to go home, I kept throwing up in the car. It was so bad that we had to stop at a car wash and wash the car.

After that we went to my friend's house so I could get some clothes to wear since mine were covered in vomit. I knew I was really drunk when I walked into my mom's house. She was up waiting for me, and I had to sit down and talk to her for a few minutes before going to bed. I have no doubt that most people would've known that I was drunk, but my mom chose either to ignore it, or she was just that naïve.

The following morning I threw up again, and my mom thought I had the flu. She tried to wake me up to go to work because I couldn't miss work. I did make it in, but I got sick and had to come home. This became a pattern for me: binge drink, get sick, repeat. Most people learn after they become sick (because it's no fun), and they'll stop or cut back on drinking, but I never learned. The moment I took one sip of alcohol, my goal would be to get drunk as fast I could so that my pain would disappear.

My high school days were filled with many parties and getting drunk. I continued to escape life via alcohol. I also learned to escape by having sex with my first boyfriend, who was two years older than me. I started dating him when I was fifteen, and we started having sex soon after. We were inseparable. He became my whole world. We would sneak away and have sex whenever we could—one time even in a corner of our high school during track practice.

I was afraid to say no even though I was scared we'd get caught. I believed that if I was in love I couldn't say no. I never truly enjoyed sex unless I was drunk. Sex was painful for me in many ways, as it triggered the sexual abuse I had experienced, along with the horrible fear and disgust I felt afterward. But I continued to do it in order to keep my boyfriend so I wouldn't feel rejected and alone.

I'd often go to his house and spend time with his family because I didn't want to be with my own family. He was my first love, and I was devastated when he eventually left me for another girl right before I went to college. I was in so much pain that cried myself to sleep one afternoon at my dad's house and actually dreamt it was the end of the world, and Jesus was coming back. I had so much rejection and abandonment in my life that I didn't know if my heart could take anymore pain.

This event marked the end of my trust in people. My dad left us emotionally for Mary, my mom had abandoned us for her boyfriend with whom she was having an affair, and my first love left me for someone else. The thought of giving any more of my love and heart away was too much. I vowed that I would never trust people again. I decided that I needed to continue to numb myself with alcohol, which continued into my college years.

New Place, Same Me

Besides self-injury and alcohol, I had found another way to escape my pain, only this time it was healthy. I was so excited to receive a letter from a small university in Michigan offering me the opportunity to run track for them. I had finished eighth in the Michigan State Track Championships for the 100-meter dash my senior year of high school, and I was now being contacted by some colleges who were interested in having me run for them. This university offered me a track scholarship, which I accepted. I was excited to be heading off on a new adventure.

My drinking, however, continued throughout my college years; in fact, it escalated. I'd often go to track meets, having eaten almost nothing all day then head back to campus to party with the rest of the team. I quickly became so drunk, I couldn't function. I became known as the one who always got sick with hangovers. Whenever I took a sip I couldn't stop. One drink was never enough. I had to get to where I couldn't feel the emotional pain any longer.

One time after a track meet, a friend and I drank about thirteen shots of whiskey in a row, and then we wandered to all the guys' dorm rooms. Fortunately, my friend Tom followed us around to make sure we were safe. I don't remember much about what happened that night except I ended up sleeping with Tom and feeling dizzy and sick. Tom soon became another escape for me, and we often had sex together from then on. I was typically drunk at the time.

I learned to live life by escaping in whatever ways I could find: alcohol, sports, sex, self-injury, and so on. I never learned how to deal with my painful emotions. However, in the midst of my pain and broken heart, I met a wonderful man who would show me what it's like to be truly loved, nurtured, and cared for.

CHAPTER 4

MEETING CLAUDE

While at college, I had decided to get a degree in French because I thought I wanted to be a teacher. I purposely sought out French foreign exchange students to learn more about their country and practice their language. During my freshman year, I bonded with all of the French students, helping them whenever I could and gaining their help in return. There were four students—all guys—and we all became good friends.

But then, when I was a sophomore, I met another French student named Claude. I will never forget seeing Claude from afar. I had known he was one of the foreign exchange students because I asked around and was told about him. I knew I had to introduce myself, even though I was intimidated.

"Hello, my name is Nichole, and I heard that you're one of the French foreign exchange students this year," I said shyly.

"Yes, I am," he replied, puffing on a cigarette. "It is a pleasure to meet you," he added with a very heavy French accent, as he held out his hand to greet me. At that moment I realized two things: I absolutely adored his accent, and I was attracted to him as more than just a new friend. The problem was, he had a girlfriend back in France, and I had a boyfriend on campus.

I was very amused by Claude's accent and the cute English mistakes he'd make. I spent time in his dorm, and we had fun together. One night, I went to a club with some friends, and Claude happened to be there as well with the other French students. He asked me to dance a slow dance with him, and we were obviously attracted to each other. At the end of the evening, we kissed goodnight.

I broke up with my boyfriend, and he broke up with his girlfriend. Claude treated me like a queen and took care of me. Although this is something I had craved my whole life, it was foreign to me, and I wasn't sure how to act. I was scared of being rejected again, but I couldn't resist the love I felt for Claude. Even though I still guarded my heart, experiencing genuine love and care from Claude was slowly allowing me to let down some of my walls and learn to trust again.

As we continued to grow closer, Claude saw my severe addiction to alcohol and was concerned for me. He decided to confront me at a party where I was drinking. I had just competed at a track meet, and, as usual, we had a party afterward. This time, there was a beer bong, which I had experience using from my high school party days. I was the only girl brave enough to do this with the guys at the party.

Claude watched in horror as his girlfriend consumed a huge amount of alcohol within seconds. I became drunk as usual, and Claude expressed his concern about my drinking. At the time, I thought he was the one with the problem since he was one of the few not drinking and getting drunk. I received what he said to me because I loved him, and I cut back on drinking, although

I never completely stopped. I couldn't imagine my life without alcohol. To stop drinking was not an option. I needed it. I had to have it in order to survive, or so I thought.

Married Life

After spending a year abroad, Claude had to return to France. This was really hard for me, as we were in love and didn't want to be apart. In addition, I had to go back home and split time between my mom and dad's house over the summer. I didn't like being back home. I ended up returning to my waitressing job in order to earn enough money to study abroad. I also decided that one way or the other, I would study abroad the following year at Claude's university so we could be together.

While we were apart, I lived in constant fear that he would break up with me, and I would be rejected again. I just couldn't accept the fact that there were some safe people who actually did love me and who would prove it by their actions. There were people who showed consistent love for me, which was new to me. I had to learn to receive this kind of love, but it wasn't easy.

After working out some issues regarding my track scholarship, I was able to spend my junior year of college abroad in Lille, France. I sat on the plane with another girl from college with whom I'd be living. I was excited and nervous at the same time, thinking of the adventure that awaited me. I also had learned that there was basically no drinking age in France, so I'd be able to buy and drink as much alcohol as I wanted. This definitely made me happy!

Spending time in France allowed me to grow in many ways—the hard way. I quickly realized that although I took three years of French in high school and another two years in college, it wasn't enough to speak and comprehend the language. Claude was helpful in finding me and the other girl an apartment and setting up our utilities and other basic necessities, but he was often in Paris on the weekends. This meant we had to figure things out on our own.

Just ordering coffee in a restaurant forced me to be courageous and step out of my comfort zone. I came to terms with the fact that I had two options: learn French by making mistakes, or stay in my apartment and be miserable. I decided to face my fears, and as a result, I made quite a few friends. Of course, whenever we partied and got drunk, there was no language barrier!

Claude and I became inseparable in France. Since he had his own apartment, I ended up living there with him more than in my own apartment. He continued to take care of me and treated me like royalty. I had never been treated that way in my entire life. I felt genuinely loved for the first time. It was amazing and scary all at the same time. But I still couldn't shake the gnawing questions in the back of my mind: "What if he abandons me? How will I survive?" I knew my heart couldn't endure any more pain, but I loved Claude, so I decided to take the risk.

After dating for a couple of years, Claude and I became engaged in a French castle. It was very romantic. When he put the ring on my finger, I felt like I was wanted for the first time. I looked to him as my hero who would fill the void in my life. In a way, he became like my god, since I had moved very far away from the real God. I had so much guilt for all the sins I was committing. I lived with Claude before being married, frequently got drunk, didn't go to church, and didn't seek God in any way. I knew God had to be mad at me, so I was afraid of Him.

Claude and I eventually moved back to the suburbs of Chicago and found a small apartment. He was required by the French government to perform military service, but he was able to fulfill that service by working at a French company near Chicago. He made minimum wage, but we were so happy to be together that the money didn't matter. I commuted to a local college to finish my degree and waitressed in order to help pay the bills. We were in love and happy.

We were soon married and continued to live in the small apartment until I graduated from college. After my graduation, we moved to downtown Chicago and lived in a high-rise apartment on the twentieth floor. In some ways, it was a dream come true. Claude was hired at the same company where he did his military service, and I worked at a French bank. We made a lot of French friends while we lived downtown, and we often had dinner parties and other get-togethers. Of course, I loved drinking wine whenever I could!

At this point in my life, I felt as though I was living in a fairy tale. I was married to a French man who adored me, we had lots of wonderful friends, I could walk to my job in downtown Chicago and experience this beautiful city every day, and we lived in a high-rise apartment with a spectacular view of downtown. Everything was perfect.

CHAPTER 5

OUR FAMILY

A couple of years after Claude and I were married, I was diagnosed with endometriosis. Endometriosis is a painful disorder where tissue that normally lines the inside of the uterus grows outside the uterus. Before my diagnosis, I had various issues as a result of the condition for several years, and the doctors couldn't determine why. I was given natural treatments that never worked. We didn't have a lot of money, so it was quite an investment to continually go to the doctor, purchase medications and tests, then never receive any answers.

Finally, a surgeon in downtown Chicago performed a laparoscopy to determine my diagnosis. He lasered some of the tissue off, but part of it still remained on my ureter. Although I was only twenty-two years old, he suggested I try to get pregnant early if I wanted to have kids. He gave me three months of shots that caused me to have hot flashes in order to try to stop the cells from growing. I hated having hot flashes and other hormonal symptoms at such a young age.

The worst part was that my only dream in life was to become a mother. In some subconscious way, I believe that one reason I wanted to have kids so desperately is so I could smother them with love and give them the childhood I had always wanted but didn't have.

Our First Child

"No way!" I exclaimed to Claude. "It says I'm pregnant!"

Not long after having the surgery, I actually became pregnant. The plan was to have fertility treatments when I wanted to get pregnant, but it happened before the treatments began. I didn't believe I was pregnant at first, so I took several more tests before going back to the doctor. One of the first things I remember thinking after I found out I was pregnant was, *Oh my goodness! I wonder how much alcohol I drank. I wonder if I put my baby in danger and maybe caused birth defects.* Fear gripped my heart until we went to the doctor and heard the baby's heartbeat for the first time.

During the months that I was pregnant, I read every book imaginable in order to be a "good mom." I wanted my child to have a better life than I had. I'll never forget seeing Claude's eyes fill with tears when Tiphanie was born. He was so proud and happy to be a father. To this day, his girls are wrapped around his finger, and he's the most amazing father I've ever seen. It's been wonderful for me watching him be a dad because it's given me a picture of what a normal, healthy father acts like.

Once Tiphanie was born, she became my whole life. I would take her on walks in the stroller, turn on classical music for her, read books to her, buy her organic milk and baby food whenever possible (which wasn't easy to find back then), take her to play groups, and enroll her in activities. Tiphanie started life with parents who loved and adored her, provided for her every need when possible, and bathed her in love and affection. We tried to be the best parents possible.

A New Adventure

With Claude and Tiphanie in my life, I finally felt a sense of stability. Then, out of the blue, Claude nervously asked me, "How would you like to move to England for a couple of years?" After moving with my mom several times and going back and forth to two different houses as a child, it felt good to finally have my own stable home. Also, we had built some wonderful friendships in Chicago and had grown to love city life. It was a very difficult decision for me, but Claude explained that we could live in a nice house in a little village in England, and the move would be a great opportunity for his career. I accepted the move because I wanted what was best for him and our family.

Deep sadness engulfed me when we had a going-away party with our friends. To me, this was just another chapter of loss in my life. It had become a pattern of getting to know people and developing a love and a bond with them, and then the next thing I knew, they'd be out of my life. I know it's normal for people to come and go, but for me, it was traumatic, as I never dealt with the pain of my past.

Reality hit hard when the moving company came to pack our belongings and put everything in a container to be sent overseas. There was no turning back now. I had to be strong and not fall apart. Over time, I had learned to "suck it up" and deal with things; sometimes we have no other choice. Besides, I had told Claude I would move, so I needed to stick to my word.

Once we arrived in England, I was quite excited about moving into our new house. Claude and I acted enthusiastic in front of

Tiphanie, who was seventeen months old. We showed her her new big room, which she was happy about, after having a tiny room in our Chicago apartment.

Later that evening, however, after all the activity had died down, I couldn't hold it together any longer. I started crying uncontrollably because I missed "home" and my friends. I suddenly felt the impact of living in a foreign country that I knew nothing about and where I didn't know a soul. I had lived in France for a couple of years, so I knew I could adapt, but the reality that we were all alone was too much for me to bear.

To make matters worse, our first week there, Claude had to travel for several days on business. Tiphanie and I were all alone. I had to learn to drive on the opposite side of the road and learn how to drive a manual transmission car, shifting gears with my left hand, since the driver sits on the right. I also had to repent from swearing many times during those first days of learning to drive in England. I was upset that I had agreed to move there. With only one car, I was left stranded when Claude needed it to drive to the airport. I felt alone and didn't know what I'd do in case of an emergency.

The Emergency

"Tiphanie, are you okay?" I screamed at my daughter. Tiphanie's car seat was sitting next to the back sliding glass door. She was rocking in it while I was in the same room with her. Before I could tell her to stop, she had crashed through the glass door in her car seat, shattering the door. Glass flew everywhere, and I was terrified that Tiphanie was seriously injured with glass shards. She cried as I frantically examined her body. Miraculously, she had no cuts at all.

I was so relieved, until I realized that I had to get the door fixed, and because Claude was out of town, I had no idea what to do or whom to call. And, this is way before Google or even cell phones! It was late in the afternoon, and all of the stores were closing. After cleaning glass off of Tiphanie and the floor, I tried to reach Claude. I was so grateful that my daughter wasn't hurt, but I reeled with anxiety about the situation.

Claude helped me find someone who was able to fix our door that night. I had always been scared to sleep alone when Claude was out of town, but it was worse when we lived in a house instead of a high rise. I wouldn't have felt safe sleeping in a new house in a foreign country with our door broken.

After Tiphanie went to sleep that night, I cried again. I felt so alone. I knew I needed to start meeting people and vowed that I would force myself to do so. I retrieved a hard cider from the fridge and started drinking. This was becoming my nightly routine, especially when Claude was traveling. I didn't get drunk that night, but I used alcohol to quench my anxiety and deal with the horrible event of the day. I never needed a reason to drink; I just knew that I needed to.

Alexia Rose

While in England, Claude and I had agreed to try to have another baby. Because of the endometriosis issues in the past, and not being able to get pregnant for a while, I decided to see a specialist, who put me on a fertility drug called Clomid. After several months, I found out I was pregnant with our second child, and we were thrilled.

By now, I had met a group of four other moms, and we regularly had play dates with our children. One mother was from Australia, one was from South Africa, one was from the United States, and the other was from England. We had a lot of fun together, and life started to feel somewhat normal for me once again.

Being pregnant was one of the happiest times in my life. The only thing that was hard for me was to stop drinking during those periods. Other than that, I was so careful with what I ate and did. I tried to protect the babies inside of me and read everything there was to read on how they were developing at each stage.

I didn't find out the sex of this baby, but I was convinced it was a boy. I was wrong. In downtown London on June 6, 1997, we welcomed our second little girl into the world. We named her Alexia Rose. Claude's mom had come from France to help us, and we saw his family rather frequently while we lived in England. In fact, Tiphanie was bilingual at one point, able to understand and speak both English and French. We were so proud to have a bilingual daughter!

Back to the States

After a couple of years of living in England, the time came for us to move back to the United States, as Claude's job required him to return to Chicago. Alexia was now ten months old, and after much research, we moved to the wonderful, family-friendly town of Naperville, Illinois. As we walked into our new house, I was thrilled to have a beautiful home with a big yard. At the same time, I was sad to leave the friends that I learned to love in England. Once again, loss became an unwelcome companion.

I had almost wanted to go back to England, which shocked me. I wasn't looking forward to starting all over and meeting new people again in America. In some ways, I hated change. Even so, life eventually seemed to be getting back to normal, and I was enjoying having a home that I could call my own for the first time in my life. It was finally a safe place for me to be.

I loved my home. I decorated our house nicely, and made sure that our yard always looked immaculate. One day I asked a couple of guys in our neighborhood how to fertilize our lawn, as they prided themselves on being "lawn experts." Whenever a challenge presented itself to me, I'd try my best to succeed at it. Fertilizing our lawn was a challenge for me, yet I wanted everything to be perfect on the outside, knowing that inside I was much less than perfect.

I figured if I kept the outside perfect, people wouldn't know how unlovable I really was. So I diligently strived to always have the perfect, spotless house and the perfect, luscious green grass. After mastering the fertilizing, the neighborhood guys told me my lawn was much greener than theirs, and they joked about how they should have never have taught me how to do it.

It proved to me how I could go all out when I wanted to. I had to show our neighbors that even though we were first-time home owners, and they were all experienced, we could become successful at home ownership as well. As far as anyone knew, I was a wonderful wife and mother with a family that was living the American dream. I was a stay-at-home mom, and my husband had a great job. We had the nice house, the white fence, the wonderful children, and no financial worries.

As much as I dreaded having to meet new people again, I knew I had to get to know some mothers in the neighborhood so our kids could play together. I met two women on my street, and we became very close. Our kids played while we chatted and had fun hanging out. We also loved to drink wine together sometimes in the early evenings, while the kids played in the backyard and before our husbands came home for dinner. It was nice having friends who lived on my street.

Unexpected Loss

Things were going well, and Claude and I decided we wanted another baby. I absolutely adored my children and tried to the best of my ability to always give them my full attention and take care of their needs. The problem was that we never knew when I would get pregnant because of my past fertility issues. One day, I decided to take a pregnancy test, and it read positive.

We were excited, although I panicked like I did with our first two children, as I wondered, *How much did I drink?* That was always my first thought when getting pregnant. I knew I had been drinking and most likely crossed the line and got drunk during the time I became pregnant. At that point in my life, I was a functioning alcoholic, but I could never imagine my life without alcohol.

In fact, one day a thought occurred to me, causing me great distress: *I wonder what I'll do in heaven if I can't drink.* Even after this thought, I was still in denial that I had a problem.

Claude and I told everyone about our pregnancy early on. I stopped drinking immediately and started taking vitamins and made sure I was eating properly. However, one day, about ten weeks into my pregnancy, I started bleeding and knew immediately I had a problem. I was scared and didn't want to lose my baby. I called my doctor, who instructed me to go to the ER. There, we learned that we had, in fact, lost our baby. I cried as they performed the ultrasound, which confirmed that our baby, who was so dearly wanted, was no longer alive. I had desperately hoped that it was all a bad dream and I would soon wake up, but it was reality.

When we arrived home, I shoved the pain inside like always, and the first thing I said was, "At least I can drink now." I was happy that I could drink to cover the pain of yet another loss in my life. I also believed it was my fault that I lost the baby. If only I had done this and that, but especially, if only I hadn't drunk alcohol, the baby would've survived. I carried guilt for years that it was my fault that we lost our precious baby. I didn't know how to cope with pain and negative feelings. I didn't know how to talk about personal issues. I kept it all inside because that's all I knew to do.

Everything I did, I strived to do with excellence and wanted it to be perfect. In addition to keeping my home spotless, I enjoyed cooking. I especially loved to cook French meals and make Claude happy by having a gourmet meal waiting for him.

I enjoyed trying to be the perfect wife and mother, yet I was also motivated by subconsciously believing if I wasn't perfect and if Claude knew the "real" me, he'd leave me or find another woman who was better.

Another area in which I excelled was throwing the most amazing birthday parties for my kids. I dove into every detail, including themed birthday cakes and matching napkins and plates. From outward appearances, I was a "super mom," and had it all together. Inside, however, I felt very much alone. I hated being alone; it was hard for me to not be around people. Whenever I was alone, even if I just went to the store on the weekends while Claude watched the kids, I couldn't stay out too long because I missed my family. I found it quite depressing to be alone, as it meant having to listen to the tormenting thoughts that plagued my mind.

A Beautiful Surprise

"I'm pregnant!" I eagerly announced to Claude after reading my pregnancy test. Approximately six months after my miscarriage, I was elated to once again be pregnant. My excitement quickly turned to worry, as I wondered if this baby would make it. I hoped that I didn't cause any harm to my child. As before, once I found out I was pregnant, I stopped drinking.

Since I could now no longer escape with alcohol, I was forced to escape in other ways. I had a hard time sitting still and relaxing. Even while pregnant with my third child, I would constantly repaint the walls. I'd get an idea about a wall color, and I'd be at the paint store within the hour, then stay up sometimes until

3:00 A.M. painting. My husband never knew what color the walls would be when he got home! For me, once I started thinking about something, I couldn't get that thought out of my mind until I did something about it. I thought this was perfectly normal.

Once, when I was eight months pregnant, I chopped down thick brush in our yard. Our yard was in the back of a sod farm that was not yet developed, and I hated the weeds and branches that blocked my view. I spent hours in the hot sun, chopping the brush. My neighbors asked if I was drinking energy drinks! They saw the manic behavior that was beginning to develop in my life, such as not being able to sit still, even while pregnant and in pain.

I had suffered from panic attacks while pregnant, but at the time I didn't realize what they were. They would hit at various times, forcing me to lie down. They were scary, but I never told anyone about them. As usual, I locked it inside and dealt with it. My life was starting to spiral out of control and fall apart because I could no longer keep everything inside.

At the time, I wasn't too concerned because I wanted to focus on my baby. Claude and I had decided that this time we would find out if we were having a boy or girl. I really believed we were having another girl, although I didn't care one way or the other. I loved my girls and grew up with all sisters. Our girls were Daddy's girls, so Claude was also fine with another one.

As soon as the ultrasound technician put the probe on me, she showed us on the screen that we were having a boy. I started laughing and almost fell off of the table. The baby looked healthy and all was well. Later that day, I went to buy a baby boy outfit. It soon hit us that we didn't know how to raise a boy! Claude and I looked at each other and said, "What are we going to do?"

The moment Lucas was born, we fell in love with him, and raising a boy became perfectly natural to us. Secretly, I had always wanted five children, so that meant we still had two to go! I loved having my babies. I didn't enjoy the lack of sleep, but the joy they brought made it all worth while. Even though I was never breast fed as a baby, I knew it was the best thing for all of my children.

I wanted to do everything perfectly. I had to give them a good life — the best life possible. After nursing my babies for two months each, I'd always stop so that I could start drinking again. It was too hard not being able to drink as much as I wanted, and I didn't want to harm my kids.

I found my life to be more difficult with three children. When Lucas was born, Tiphanie was almost six, and Lexy was three. It's normal for a mom to feel overwhelmed at times, and we were on our own, not having any family nearby. My family lived in Michigan, and Claude's family lived in France. But, we now had a new family — our church family.

Awhile before Lucas was born, Claude and I had decided that we needed to start going to church. After trying several churches, we finally found one that we both agreed on. Initially, we'd listen to the sermon then immediately leave. We never made an effort to get to know anyone. I found out later that one person from the church thought of us as the "hermit family."

Eventually, we attended a home group fellowship with other couples and got to know them personally. I had started attending the church's weekly Bible study as well and determined that I wanted to grow spiritually. I knew I needed God, but I had so many questions, I didn't know where to start. I was always afraid of God and knew I could never live up to His standards in the Bible. Yet, for Claude and I, we wanted to do the right thing and take our children to church every week.

We didn't realize it at the time, but soon our new church family would be rallying around us in a big way. God knew all along, and He perfectly planned for them to be in our lives at just the right time.

Living It Up in France

"We need to go to France to see my family," Claude told me unexpectedly one day. This was fine with me, as I loved visiting Paris, even though I knew it would be difficult to fly with three young children. I started getting excited about our trip. I decided to take a pregnancy test before going, as I was very irregular with my monthly cycles. I thought it had been awhile since my last period, and I needed to know either way. I wanted to know if I'd be able to take advantage of the unlimited supply of fine wine his parents would have during their meals. I was happy to partake of the good wine they served!

The family joke was, "Nichole doesn't need water; she has wine." It was true that I didn't drink water during meals. I only drank wine, especially when it was acceptable and everyone was participating. With Claude's family, I could drink as much as I wanted, and it wouldn't be frowned upon. And, no one would know how much I was drinking because everyone was so engrossed in the table conversation. I could remain quiet, especially due to the language barrier, and just sit back and drink.

I was relieved when I learned I wasn't pregnant. Now, I could really live it up in France, and that's just what I did. We had a wonderful time during our stay, and shortly after arriving home, I took another pregnancy test, as I still hadn't started my period. To my horror, it was positive. I took another test to confirm, but the results were the same.

I was scared about how much alcohol I had been consuming. As soon as I found out, I immediately stopped drinking and again started taking my vitamins and watching my diet. I was nervous and excited about welcoming our fourth child into our beautiful family. I didn't care how hard it would be to raise four children with no family around; I knew we'd somehow manage.

At about ten weeks into my pregnancy, I started bleeding and panicked. *I can't lose this baby!* I thought. *If I lose this baby, I know without a shadow of a doubt it's my fault. I will have murdered my baby.* We went to the ER to once again witness the devastation of realizing there was no heartbeat. Another baby gone. I started weeping in the ER. The pain was unbearable.

After I gained some composure, the thought came back to me, *At least I can drink, and at this point, I need to drink. I can't handle this pain.* From that point, I drank so I could feel the effect of the alcohol numbing my pain, yet I was still able to function. When Claude and I went to restaurants with friends, I'd get nearly drunk. I'd keep myself together and not wobble as I walked. No one suspected that I had a problem.

PART II

TROUBLING TRANSFORMATION

CHAPTER 6

FALLING APART

Not long after my second miscarriage, a friend came to visit me. She had suffered with a few miscarriages, and when she saw me acting as though my miscarriages were no big deal and I told her that at least I could drink again, she became concerned. I'll never forget her words of warning: "If you keep stuffing things in and numbing yourself, your life will eventually fall apart."

I remembered those words, but in my heart, I didn't believe them. Yet, as time went on, I started becoming irritable for no reason. I also began having flashbacks of sexual abuse. This shocked me. To block the pain from the realization that someone who was supposed to take care of me violated me instead, my daily drinking increased. As a parent, I could never imagine abusing my kids, especially sexually. The reality hit me how traumatizing it was to be violated as an innocent child and trapped, with no way out. It disturbed me to the point where I started having anger problems that I couldn't manage.

One time, something very minor triggered me, and I threw pots and pans in the kitchen. My kids weren't around, but I still felt guilty after that. This episode only confirmed that I was a bad, unlovable person who was unworthy of love. I knew anger was a sin, but I just kept on sinning. Why couldn't I get it together? What was wrong with me?

I had been dealing with so much loss in my life, but what I was about to hear was, in many ways, the straw that broke the camel's back. My two best friends in the neighborhood told me within two weeks of each other that they were both moving out of state. I started sobbing when I heard the news. Not one, but both of them were leaving me. Not again!

I had finally bonded with people who had become like family, and they were leaving me. I loved my friends from church, but these two women were my best friends. Our children, who frequently got together for play dates, had also bonded with one another. I started falling apart and could no longer control it.

I began drinking stronger alcohol and couldn't wait for the clock to hit 5:00 every night. To me, if I started drinking then, it meant I didn't have a problem. At the same time, I knew my life was unraveling on the inside, and I began to deal with depression and anger at the same time. *What do I do with this?* I asked myself. I had no idea how to handle the pain I felt. It seemed like alcohol couldn't even numb it anymore. I knew I couldn't keep shoving all my emotions inside; it was no longer working. I was a volcano ready to erupt. I didn't know when it would happen, but I knew that eventually the eruption would occur, as something was desperately wrong.

A Cry for Help

At this point I did something very out of the ordinary. I invited my pastor over and talked to him about the sexual abuse of my past and what was currently happening in my life. I was crying out for help. Asking for help was difficult for me, as I always had to do things on my own. I never received help for anything as a child. I learned to deal with things by myself. But now, flashbacks were taking a toll on me, and my daily use of alcohol was starting to scare me.

The pressure of having to maintain a perfect appearance on the outside added to the stress. My outside definitely did not match my inside. Externally, things looked wonderful, while internally, I screamed, "You're anything but perfect. You're an unworthy failure. People are going to find out who you really are."

My pastor was encouraging and loving toward me. Because of the sexual abuse, I had a hard time trusting men, even the husbands of my friends. All men made me anxious, so to be comfortable with my pastor was surprising to me. I hadn't planned on it, but as he was about to leave, I admitted to him that I was drinking alcohol daily, and it concerned me. He encouraged me to talk to his wife, Ingrid.

I had known that Ingrid was a previous alcoholic and had endured the shame of her addiction in front of the church. I also knew she went to rehab to get help, and it changed her life. I had always loved our pastors and enjoyed having company, but I used to think, *We can't have them over because they don't drink.* I had confided in her husband, Pastor Fred, because of her past problem with alcohol. When Fred left my house that night, I assured him that I would talk to her, even though I was afraid.

Little did any of us know that right around the corner lay a roller coaster full of years of pain and turmoil. The devastation would ultimately cause us to become very close friends. And, it would show me that not everyone ends up leaving me. I discovered that there are those in this world who are capable of loving with the genuine and unconditional love of Christ.

It Can't Be True!

"I feel like I'm dying inside. I would love to talk to you sometime," read the note that I'd slipped Ingrid in the church nursery not long after meeting with Fred. For the first time in my life, I was learning how to be vulnerable with people. Even though I had trust issues my whole life, I'd seen the integrity that my friends had in our church, and I knew I could trust them with my heart. I had no other way to describe how I was feeling. It truly felt like I was dying inside.

Ingrid read the note, and with tears in her eyes, she came over and hugged me. She said she would love to talk to me, so we scheduled a time for later that week. I left church feeling afraid of our meeting, yet excited at the same time. Could someone finally help me with the pain that I didn't know how to deal with on my own? I believed she could help me with the drinking problem I knew I had but was too scared to admit to anyone. If I did admit it, I would have to stop drinking. I didn't think I could live my life without alcohol. I had already let that cat out of the bag to some extent when I spoke with Fred, and I was certain he had told Ingrid.

Later that week, I sat in my family room with Ingrid and poured my heart out to her, telling her all about my drinking. "I believe you are an alcoholic," she said to me bluntly, yet lovingly. *Alcoholic!* I knew I didn't like that label, but I also knew she must be right. She asked if we could pour out all the wine that was in my fridge, along with the unopened bottles throughout my house.

Claude and I had just gone to the wine store the week before and purchased a case of really good, expensive wine. As I watched it swirl down the drain, I was saddened and thought, *What have I done? Why did I share this? Why was I so vulnerable?* It was too late. The wine was gone. There was no longer a way of escape in my house. Before Ingrid left, she told me to tell Claude that I was an alcoholic. It was important for me to admit it out loud. Even though the thought of that was terrifying to me, I agreed to do it.

I remember telling Claude that night that I had something important to tell him. I shared with him what happened with Ingrid that day, and I told him I believed I may be an alcoholic. Stunned, he responded, "There's no way you're an alcoholic. That can't be true. Sure, you like to drink, but I don't see you getting drunk all the time." He didn't realize that I was a functioning alcoholic and that I was now drinking stronger alcohol because I felt like I needed to.

"I Am an Alcoholic"

One day, shortly before meeting with Pastor Fred and Ingrid, I was making dinner and took a hard cider out of the fridge to drink it. At that moment, the thought occurred to me, *Why do I need to drink this?* I couldn't answer that question, so I blocked the thought out of my mind and drank it anyway. I didn't want to accept in any way that I had a problem with drinking. When Claude denied what I said, I told myself, "Maybe he's right. Maybe I don't have a problem." I had promised Ingrid that I wouldn't drink anymore, and at the time, I honestly thought I could do it. I just thought, *OK, I'm an alcoholic. I'll just suck it up and not drink.* In some ways, I thought I could handle it—on my own—like I did everything else.

I got through my first day without a drink. But then, when I awoke the next morning, I could barely move. I felt the most pain I had ever felt in my whole life at that moment. I was trembling and shaking from not drinking the day before, and I literally felt like a freight train hit me head-on. I didn't know what to do. By this time, I was down to the lowest weight I had ever been. I had been losing weight for a while, but the depression and drinking caused me to become the thinnest I had ever been in my life.

My life was truly starting to fall apart. Even my outside life was starting to match what was going on inside of me. I was way too thin, and people could tell. The words that my friend had said to me earlier about my life falling apart were coming to pass. At this moment in my life, I felt a pain that was completely foreign to me, and I couldn't numb it. I said I wouldn't drink anymore; I gave my word.

As I tried to get ready for the day and couldn't do it, I finally called my pastor to tell him that I didn't understand what I was feeling and that I wasn't doing well. He tried to encourage me the best he could. As I continued throughout my day, I had remembered that we were invited to our neighbor's house that night to have dinner, and I was the one responsible for bringing the wine. *Now what am I going to do? How am I going to handle this?* I decided that we couldn't cancel and that somehow I could handle it. I was determined to be strong and not give in to drinking. I would bring the wine, and I'd be fine.

As the day progressed, I could still feel my life unraveling and knew I needed to hide it from my neighbors. It didn't work, and they could tell I wasn't myself. They sensed something was wrong, but as usual, I pretended like everything was fine. At about 4:30, they asked if they could crack open the wine I brought. I told them yes because I'd never had a problem with it before. "I'm not going to be drinking tonight," I told them, to their surprise.

As soon as the bottle was opened and the wine was poured, I couldn't stop obsessing about having some. I don't even remember the conversations that night because I was in constant torment over the fact that I promised I wouldn't drink, and I knew that I could never go back to drinking the way I used to. How would I survive? I couldn't even make it one day! After about thirty minutes of vacillating over whether or not to give in, I decided to go for it. I rationalized that it was my life, and I would do what I wanted.

I reminded myself of a rebellious little girl having a temper tantrum or a baby who had its pacifier taken away. Alcohol was my comfort. It was my pacifier. In some ways, it was my lover. Oh, how I loved it! How would I ever live without it? As far as I was concerned, I couldn't. After giving in to one glass, I continued drinking, and probably had more wine than anyone else that night.

At one point during the night, I called a friend at church who I had also told about my alcohol problem. I called to tell her that I gave in and got drunk, and I was laughing about it over the phone. I told her that I didn't have a problem, but she insisted that I did. When I hung up, I knew she would tell Ingrid and Fred, so I decided I may as well go back to the party and drink some more.

Ingrid felt it would be in my best interest to start attending AA (Alcohol Anonymous) meetings. We went together on a Friday night, and she had prepared me for what we would encounter. I had wondered if I would see anyone I knew, and I imagined how embarrassing that would be. I introduced myself, followed by the phrase, "and I am an alcoholic." The term *alcoholic* became my new identity, which I hated. I only attended a few meetings then gave up.

Depression Takes Root

As time went on, I became more and more depressed. I went from having the perfect house and finding it hard to sit down and relax because there was so much I felt I needed to accomplish, to lying in a fetal position on the couch. I just lay there as my mind raced. Thoughts of depression, anxiety, torment, emptiness, sadness, and hopelessness swirled about my mind all at the same time. My body may have had rest, but my mind never did. Constant tormenting thoughts kept my mind in turmoil.

Before long, suicidal thoughts entered: *I should kill myself. I'm a failure. My kids would be better off without an alcoholic mother. I can't keep causing them pain. I should just go through with it. Life is too hard, especially without alcohol. Life is not worth living without alcohol.* This became a typical thought pattern for me, and the more I dwelled on these thoughts, naturally, the more depressed I became. It was the worst on weekends, beginning Friday night. Knowing it was Friday night and I couldn't drink was torture. It wasn't fair! Why was I always the abnormal one? Why was there always something wrong with me? I regretted ever reaching out for help and was mad at myself for doing so.

My suicidal thinking was relentless. I had absolutely no power to stop the thoughts. As I drove, I'd think about crashing into a ditch or a pole to kill myself. Throughout the day, I'd think of different ways that I would go through with ending my life.

I began seeing a Christian counselor that my church recommended. During my first session, I assured her that I didn't really need to be there and that my childhood was perfectly normal. I was in deep denial, and it took hours of counseling for the blinders to be removed so I could see what I actually endured as a child with the extremely dysfunctional family that I grew up in. I never wanted to deal with all of this, so I kept everything inside, never telling anyone until now. Even my own husband had no idea how bad it was until I began opening up to him. All of my secrets were about to be disclosed.

About six months after I spilled the beans to everyone, my support system of family and friends persuaded me to go to rehab because of my continual struggles with alcohol. I went for six weeks and bonded with the female facilitator, whom I kept in touch with after the program ended. My church friends and family came to my program graduation, expressing how proud they were of me for wanting to change my life for the better and for following through with rehab.

During the six-week program, we were assigned a lot of homework. I realized through it all how my family dynamics growing up had truly impacted me in so many ways. I discovered more about myself than I ever knew before. I also learned for the first time how to be vulnerable and real with people instead of holding everything inside. As I left the graduation ceremony, I promised to attend the weekly support meetings. My life was finally beginning to look up, as I felt as though I had help in my life and wasn't alone. The baby steps had begun.

We're Going to Disney World!

"I have a surprise for you," Claude informed me when I was nearing the end of rehab. "Our family is going to Disney World as soon as you graduate from the program."

"Really?" I asked, excitedly. I thanked Claude for planning this for us. He loved to go on vacation. We'd frequently go different places with our children and create wonderful family memories. As a child, Claude's family often vacationed together, but my family hardly went anywhere, so I wasn't used to traveling. I had loved taking vacations with Claude and our kids, but that was before my life started falling apart.

I began having some anxiety about going on vacation to Disney World, knowing that I wouldn't be able to drink alcohol. Relaxing with alcohol is something I always enjoyed, so the thought of remaining sober seemed in some ways too difficult to handle.

When I told people at rehab and some of my support friends that I would be going on vacation after graduation, they didn't think it was a good idea for me because they knew how tough it would be. But, I always loved a challenge and enjoyed proving people wrong, so I just assured everyone that I'd have a good time and would be okay.

I was planning on taking my AA "Big Book" and the little AA daily devotional with me, so I was certain I would be just fine. In addition, I'd just been put on an anti-depressant by a psychiatrist I'd seen during rehab. She had diagnosed me with depression and felt that an anti-depressant would help. I figured that would "kick in" while we were on vacation, and I'd be cured of my mental anguish. I couldn't have been more wrong.

The Fight to Stay Sober

Sitting in the restaurants at Disney World and not drinking while there was alcohol all around me was utter torment. How could so many people in AA, who claimed to be completely set free from the chains of alcoholism, have absolutely no problem being around it?

What's wrong with me? I wondered. *Why can't I experience that same freedom? How will I live life always taunted by alcohol when there's no way to escape it?* It's everywhere! It's in grocery stores, restaurants, in my friends' homes, and even at Disney World!

Here I was, in a beautiful setting with my family, and my mind started racing again. I tried to the best of my ability to stay emotionally present, but it was difficult. I loved them so much, and I was angry that I morphed from a mother who poured herself into her kids in every way possible to a person who now didn't even know how to take care of herself.

I was so absorbed in my mental torment that I couldn't function. Guilt and shame overwhelmed me. The shame I felt for being an alcoholic was unbearable; after all, I was supposed to be a better parent than my parents were. I strived to do everything opposite of my parents, yet I was struggling with an addiction myself. How did I get here? I wanted the nightmare to stop. I wanted to wake up and go back to the times when life felt normal. I wanted to go back to when I was present with my family and could have a glass of wine here and there with friends. But the reality was that my former life was over, and I could now only grieve what was lost.

While at Disney World, we decided to go on one of the most popular rides, It's a Small World. We had been to Disney World many times before, and our kids knew all the rides. We were excited to see the different countries represented in the ride, along with the catchy tune that played throughout. We climbed into our boat, and as our children pointed to different parts of the ride, screaming in excitement, my mind suddenly engaged in its own conversation:

"Am I going to relapse again?"

"No, I can't do that anymore."

"Yes, but I want to drink, and I can hide it so no one will ever know."

"No, I can't drink anymore."

"But I have to have it. I can't live without it. I'm going to relapse because I can't live like this anymore. I can do it. I can get away with it."

We were in sunny Florida, in one of the most amazing destinations for families to have fun, and I was still tormented, depressed, and obsessed with all the alcohol around me. As I watched everyone else drink, I longed to be "normal" like they were.

I couldn't tell anyone what was going on. As much as I tried to hide it, Claude knew there was something wrong. After all, he was starting to watch the person he loved and married change completely into another person whom he didn't know. It was heartbreaking for him to watch his once-vibrant, highly functioning wife evolve into a suffering fragment of herself, always lost in her own world and trapped in her own mind.

CHAPTER 7

NEXT STOP: THE PSYCH WARD

After we returned home, everything became worse. As I write this, it's all a blur, and I can't remember most of the details. But what I do remember clearly is that I continued having racing, anxiety-laden thoughts. I didn't know how to gain control over them, and thoughts of suicide became common. It wasn't long before I had relapsed on alcohol and once again spun into the downward spiral of guilt and self-condemnation. I started asking myself, "How could I relapse after going to rehab and AA and counseling and even being on medication? I'm a failure!" This relapse continued to confirm the negative conversations I had with myself about how I could never do anything right and God must've made a mistake bringing me into the world.

I truly believed that I couldn't take much more, and killing myself to end the misery for me and others looked more and more appealing. My life was truly the definition of insanity—doing the same thing over and over but expecting different results; or, in my case, thinking the same negative things over and over and expecting different results. The little joy that I felt at times could never compare to the endless torment from the onslaught of anxious thoughts.

I made a decision: I went to my kitchen, grabbed a huge butcher knife, and started cutting myself. I had retreated to my childhood behavior, but this time it was much worse. As I made cuts on my legs, I noticed that while I was feeling the pain of my skin being sliced open, my mind had temporarily stopped focusing on the evil voices in my head. I actually began to feel relaxed as I watched the blood flow.

In Sickness...

When Claude came home, he immediately knew something was wrong, but it took me awhile to admit what I had done. Claude quickly phoned our pastor, who suggested he call my counselor and talk with her. After speaking with my counselor, it was decided that I should be admitted to the psychiatric ward. I was reluctant and quite hesitant, but down deep, I knew I should go, so I agreed.

As Claude drove me there, I thought how this was certainly not in our plan as husband and wife. Yet, Claude took our wedding vows very seriously, and he was committed to stay with me through sickness and health. Arriving at the hospital, embarrassment took hold, as I had to explain to the medical receptionist that I had cut myself. I was there because I intentionally inflicted harm upon myself. It was all my fault. I knew I wasn't in my right mind, but I didn't know how to fix it.

They admitted me to the psychiatric hospital, at which point Claude had to prepare to leave me. They checked my belongings and made Claude take home everything I wasn't allowed to have, such as shoes with laces, or anything else that could be used to help me hurt myself. I felt like a little child who couldn't be trusted, even though I knew I didn't even trust myself.

Claude and I hugged and cried as we said goodbye to one another. He looked at me with eyes that said, "I so want to fix you, but I don't know how." I saw fear in his eyes as he pulled away from my embrace. Shame engulfed my very being. I experienced what I believe a lot of people do who go to a psych ward: There's relief, in a sense, to get help, but as soon as you arrive, you want out!

Day One

The next morning when I awoke, the full realization of where I was and what had happened hit me. My emotional pain was overwhelming. The doctors gave me a schedule of things that I was required to do, such as group therapy and having specific mealtimes. I didn't know a soul there, and it was all foreign to me. I definitely didn't want to be there. I wanted to be home with my family. And, I wanted to be normal again. I longed to wake up with my kids and Claude and be able to do things as a family.

Instead, my children were waking up to their father who had to explain how I was "sick" and had to go away to get help. I can only imagine their pain and confusion hearing these words. I wish I could've protected them from the sorrow, but I couldn't. I couldn't even help myself.

As I dressed for the day, feelings of loneliness and emptiness consumed every part of me. I had never experienced such depths of these emotions in my entire life. My heart was broken and crushed. Shame, guilt, and regret had become my constant companions. I knew that I would need to do whatever the doctors had asked of me because they were my only hope for being able to function once again.

As I walked into the main area of the ward, a thick cloud of oppression and sadness encroached upon me like a dark, damp winter fog. One man sat on a couch, conversing with himself, completely in his own little world. I ached as I saw him all alone, realizing how sick he was. How could I be with these people? I wasn't as sick as they were. I didn't belong here, I told myself. Surely, the doctors made a mistake. I found a comfortable spot in front of the television and waited for breakfast.

Still No Peace

During my first group therapy session, I did little more than listen to everyone else. I realized that I could relate to most of the patients in different ways. They had all been through extreme trauma and were now experiencing some of the same agonizing thoughts that I was. I felt both compassion and empathy toward them.

I continued attending the group sessions and ended up meeting a girl whom I felt comfortable talking with, which helped the time to pass. After many sessions and consulting with counselors and psychiatrists, I was discharged the following week. My diagnosis was depression, which I thought would be manageable. I began to have hope that I could experience some healing with the anti-depressant I was taking, along with sleep medication. Unfortunately, the little bit of peace and hope that I felt upon leaving the hospital didn't last.

The best part was seeing my kids and Claude again. To help me deal with the guilt of being away from home, I smothered my children with love and tried to spoil them by taking them places. I wanted to make up for being a "terrible, depressed parent." But, I found that even when we'd go places like a play place that was filled with loud noise from screaming children, my mind just became even louder, as if it was trying to compete with the joyful noises. It began wandering back to the same familiar, racing thoughts, but now it was even worse.

I'd look at the other parents around me and wonder, *What is it like to think about normal things?* Although I was going to AA and to the weekly support meeting where I attended rehab, and going to counseling, and seeing a psychiatrist, and going to church and Bible studies, it wasn't enough to stop the continuous anxious thoughts. They were like a race car going around and around a racetrack at 200 miles an hour. I didn't know how I could live the rest of my life like this, and I didn't want to do it. I started to hate myself more, if that was even possible.

CHAPTER 8

MY NEW IDENTITY

As time went on and I continued to relapse with alcohol, self-injure my body, and deal with bouts of severe depression, I finally let my psychiatrist know the extent of what was happening. She conducted various tests, ultimately diagnosing me with bipolar disorder and PTSD.

When I first heard that I had bipolar disorder, I was relieved. I felt as though I finally had an answer to what was taking place inside of me. After spending considerable time researching the disease, I realized it definitely matched what I had been experiencing. At the same time, however, I decided that I didn't like that label and was ashamed of it.

How could I be bipolar? I wondered. I told myself that the diagnosis had to be wrong. *I don't want this label for the rest of my life. What will people think of me? They'll always view me as crazy.*

The psychiatrist who diagnosed me had been referred to me through the rehab program. I decided to get a second opinion from another psychiatrist because I believed the first one made a mistake. My Christian counselor gave me the name of a well-respected Christian psychiatrist whom I saw several weeks later.

More Labels

"You're a classic bipolar case," the second psychiatrist, Dr. Brown, confirmed, looking straight into my eyes. My heart sank. There was no escaping it. This was a label I would have forever. I had read and was told that bipolar disorders are incurable and would need to be managed for the rest of my life. *This can't be my cross to bear!* I pouted to myself. I knew that I couldn't shut my mind off and that I had a brain disease, but I also knew that I needed help dealing with it because I didn't know how much longer I could live in this condition.

Dr. Brown prescribed a mood stabilizer and changed the anti-depressant I had been taking, which was causing me even more anxiety. At this point, I was on an anti-depressant, a mood stabilizer, and a sleeping medication. I figured that since this doctor was a Christian, he must be hearing from God, so surely he would know how to help me. I decided that perhaps this *was* my cross to bear so that I could help others who also struggled with this disease.

I tried to find some positive reason for being diagnosed with bipolar disorder, but it was very difficult. My new identity in life became a bipolar alcoholic with PTSD.

After a couple of days of taking the mood stabilizer, I asked my friend Ingrid, "Is this what normal people feel like?" For the first time in a very long time, I felt peace and even somewhat "normal." I was amazed and encouraged! But, the peace was only temporary. Within a few short weeks, the anguish began again.

I started experiencing uncontrollable, racing thoughts combined with mania, which is not good, especially since I was still self-injuring in order to escape my mental anxiety. I called my psychiatrist frequently so he could adjust my medications. He eventually put me on an anti-psychotic drug to take in times of crisis. Most of the time when I took it, I had even more anxiety. I went from small, temporary periods of peace to periods of mania, with a racing mind and suicidal thoughts.

Not long after this, I was diagnosed with borderline personality disorder. The list of labels was growing longer. Now I was a Christian bipolar, borderline personality, self-injuring alcoholic with PTSD. The labels only served to strengthen the negative messages I continued to write on my heart and had believed my whole life. The messages screamed, "I'm defective! I'm unlovable! I'm abnormal! There's something wrong with me." The labels proved medically that I was, in fact, crazy.

I felt like an outcast everywhere I went, and I lived in a constant state of fear of rejection. I was certain that everyone would ultimately leave me. Even though this is what I believed, the reality was very different. My pastor, his wife, and our church family continued to support and love us no matter what. They provided meals when needed, and they regularly prayed for us. Ingrid and my friend Kimm were also always right by my side.

God was showing me that there were people around me who displayed His love, but it took me years to believe that their love was truly genuine and unconditional. I believe that God had great compassion on what I was going through. He knew the root of why I had believed the lies that I was believing. His heart ached for me to know the truth of how much He and others loved me. During the most horrific and painful time of my life, His grace and mercy provided me people who would demonstrate His awesome love to me.

The Gift of Elizabeth

If someone would have brought me a genie in a bottle to grant me one wish during this time, I would've wished for peace of mind because of how tormented I was. Money meant nothing to me; in fact, we were fine financially. Claude had a wonderful corporate job in which he was quite successful. He was making a salary that most people could only dream of. Because of this, it was easy for me to see that money can't buy happiness or peace of mind.

Several months after seeing the second psychiatrist and after struggling to escape from a manic episode, my psychiatrist sent me to an outpatient program at a local hospital. He wanted me to attend all day for two weeks so I could stabilize. My son was young at the time, and I needed to take him to daycare. The guilt I felt dropping him off as he clung to me, not wanting me to leave, was unbearable. It was in moments like this when I really hated myself and believed I was a terrible mother.

It broke my heart to have to leave my son. I had raised my two daughters at home during their toddler years and gave them my full attention, but my son was missing out. My two girls were in school, but my absence after school, and having someone babysit them until I arrived home from the program was hard on them as well. I wanted to go back to my old life—back to when it seemed like I was living the dream, the time when no one knew about my diagnoses, the time when no one knew I was an alcoholic. I longed to go back, but I could not and would not.

"Nichole?" the woman asked smiling as she came to get me from the waiting room.

"Yes," I responded. I was relieved to see such a peaceful look on her face. *Maybe they can help me,* I thought. *Maybe I'll finally get some healing and peace back in my life.* I followed her into her office and learned that she would be my counselor while I was at the program and would be meeting with me frequently. As she started asking me questions, I began weeping. I knew my son wanted to be at home and not at daycare, and I had a hard time releasing the guilt. I knew it was my fault he was there.

"It's okay," Elizabeth reassured me. "You're here to help yourself. It's time to focus on you, and your son is in good hands. He'll be just fine. We want you to focus on yourself here, and we want to help you."

I'll never forget her soothing, loving voice. Elizabeth was a gift from God, and I started trusting her. As time went on in the program, she and I bonded. It was beautiful. I discovered that she was a Christian, and we talked about God often. I loved that. Whenever I was in any group therapy times—inpatient or outpatient—I'd always bring up my faith. I still had faith and hope in God. I sometimes had people come to me afterward, telling me how encouraged they were and how they were going to start focusing on their relationship with God. That always blessed me.

I used to think that maybe that was why God gave me bipolar disorder. He wanted me to share about Jesus in the therapy groups. I assumed that's why it was still my cross to bear. I believed that God gave me the disorder to give Him glory. I even had the counselors tell me that I should go into the field of counseling because they noticed that I had quite a bit of discernment and wise counsel for the other patients. This encouraged me a lot because I knew they were talking to a bipolar, borderline personality, alcoholic, self-injurer with PTSD. Maybe there was a light at the end of the tunnel. Maybe I could help people in the future.

The day came for me to leave the program, and I was extremely sad to leave Elizabeth. We exchanged contact information to keep in touch. To me, this was a huge gift from the Lord because He knew how hard it was for me to handle loss. Even though it was against the rules for her to do this, she knew she was hearing from God and that we were meant to keep in touch.

Over the years, we've talked on the phone from time to time, and we still send Christmas cards to one another. What a wonderful blessing from God to keep her in my life. Elizabeth was a fun, caring, and loving big sister to me, and God used her to continue to help me in my journey. Yet, I still had a long way to go.

Failing at AA

The peace I experienced from the outpatient program didn't last. Once again, my mind started racing, which caused me to lose hope. In an attempt to drown out the inner voices, I'd listen to really loud secular music. Sometimes I'd drive around in my car while the kids were at school, listening to Eminem and Madonna and contemplating crashing in order to kill myself.

I'd also listen to Christian music, but during times of anguish, I chose secular music. I felt as though I could relate more to those lyrics, and I experienced too much guilt hearing Christian songs. During these times, I wasn't experiencing the God that was being sung about. I could go from talking about Jesus in therapy groups to not wanting anything to do with Him and trying to hide from Him. I praise the Lord that even though I left Him, He never left me. He was always with me, always trying to speak truth to me and pursue me. He did not give up on me.

I continued to relapse on alcohol. Even though I had a sponsor and was continuing to go to different meetings, counseling, psychiatric appointments, Bible studies, and church, I still couldn't remain sober. I felt ashamed each time I went to my AA meeting and had to admit yet again that I had relapsed.

For the most part, people were supportive, and it wasn't uncommon for them to hear about others relapsing. But most of them had been sober for years, and I think they started to give up on me. I believe they thought that I'd be one of the countless numbers of people who "never get it" and end up dying of alcoholism or going to jail. The famous line was that alcoholism led to "jails, institutions, and death." Not very encouraging.

Although at first I had a hard time sharing about myself in the meetings, I learned to become vulnerable. I figured I had nothing to lose. Many people showed me unconditional acceptance, but there were some who told me that the reason I relapsed is because I must not have done a thorough enough fourth step, which includes going back and examining my life, forgiving people, and realizing the wrongs I had done to others. I had done three fourth steps by this point. I had done all of it. I had pages and pages in a journal of different fourth steps.

No, it wasn't the fourth step that was the problem. The problem was that I started to feel like a defective AA member. I couldn't even get that right! Truly, there was no getting out of it; I was a loser. I was defective and abnormal and didn't fit in anywhere. The negative heart messages were correct again. Even though I completed the ninety meetings in ninety days after most relapses, it didn't work for me. I couldn't stay sober for years as the regular members were doing.

I had done everything I was told to do in AA, including reading the Big Blue Book at home and doing the daily devotionals, but I wasn't receiving the miracles that the people in the Blue Book seemed to receive. I wasn't one of those miracle people who had the desire of alcohol taken away. If I had a magic wand, I would've waved it over me and wished that I could function without alcohol. I would've wished that as I grocery shopped and passed by the alcohol displays I wouldn't be tempted. And, I would've wished that I could go to a restaurant or a party and not have a desire to drink.

I would've wished for all these things, but I didn't have that magic wand or that miracle to help me. In fact, my friends from church enjoyed going out and drinking, and they were reluctant to invite me because they knew I had a hard time being around alcohol. I wanted to be included so I wouldn't feel rejected, but at the same time I knew I was still struggling.

One time my friends did invite me to meet them at a restaurant, where they were all drinking. I had a hard time and tried to hide it, but people could read me like a book, and I ended up leaving early. I wished that alcohol was banned from the face of the earth! I wanted it to go away, but it wouldn't. I came to the conclusion that I would be in agony for the rest of my life and forced to stay home from social settings or else hold my own parties where alcohol wasn't allowed.

I was grateful that Ingrid didn't drink, but she also didn't have a long list of relapses as I did. I had no idea why she was able to get rid of her desire for alcohol and not me. Why did it work for her? I continued to believe the voices that told me how abnormal I was. What other choice did I have?

No Way Out

Over time, I tried to accept the diagnosis of bipolar disorder. I did much research on the topic, even buying a book about depression—*Blue Genes* by Dr. Paul Meier, a well-respected Christian psychologist. One line from his book jumped out at me: "In dozens of years of treating thousands of people for bipolar illness, we do not know of a single case that God chose to heal" (Tyndale House Publishers, 2005, 197).

As I read these words, I had completely lost any remaining hope that I may've had, even though I already knew that bipolar disorder was incurable. I had heard that from my psychiatrist, my therapist, the inpatient and outpatient programs, other psychiatrists who helped me, and through my research. Still, reading those words were a slap in my face, driving home the reality that I'd never be healed and that I'd live with torment off and on my whole life.

What I didn't understand was why God chose to do great miracles in the Bible, yet He wanted me to live with mental anguish. I had heard of people being healed of cancer and other diseases, so why not mental illness? Was it too difficult for God? It just didn't make sense to me, and I wasn't sure that I truly trusted and wanted a relationship with a God who wanted me to suffer with mental torment in order to give Him glory.

In the same book, the author mentioned how he sold a special vitamin drink specifically aimed at helping those who were bipolar. I'd do anything to attain any measure of peace in my life, so I looked into it. It was very expensive, but I decided I needed to try it. The cost was worth any peace I could receive. When I finally received it and measured out the right amount, I hesitated. I knew it wouldn't taste good, but it was worth the sacrifice. I gulped it down as fast as possible. It was disgusting, but I had to be strong and choke it down. The label listed a concoction of about fifty different vitamins, and I wondered, *Is this going to finally help me?*

I found out rather quickly that the answer was no. It didn't help me at all, and I felt scammed. But then I reasoned that it was probably just me again and maybe it actually does work for other people. Not only did I have agonizing thoughts, but I also had regular thoughts of self-pity. The longer I dwelled on such things, the more negative my emotions became. My life was a continual roller coaster and unfortunately, there was no way off the ride!

CHAPTER 9

PROGRESSIVE SELF-HARM

Although I continued to try to be the best wife and mother I could, it seemed that my manic depressive episodes were becoming worse and worse. I still self-harmed with knives from time to time but always managed to hide it. My strategy was to self-injure in places that no one would see. I lived in a nice neighborhood, and I knew some gossip had started about me, so I couldn't afford to add more fuel to the fire.

Still, I decided I needed to cut myself deeper because the knives were only literally scratching the surface. So, I took apart one of my razors and used its blade to inflict more pain and blood faster than a knife ever could. The first time I began rubbing the razor across my body in different ways, I experienced peace while I physically felt pain. I had a stash of gauze with me and continued wiping the blood away.

I believed I could only survive the insecurities, self-hatred, and hidden secrets I'd stuffed inside by harming myself. I also believed that the pain of the trauma and abuse I endured during my childhood could only be temporarily soothed if I hurt myself physically. I couldn't stop this continuous cycle.

Eventually, I went from cutting various hidden parts of my body to cutting my wrists. I had become so tormented, I didn't care who saw it. I figured I could still learn to hide it by making just a small slice so it wouldn't be obvious. There were many times when I wondered if I would actually hit a main artery. Deep down, I wished that I would. After all, if I died, at least I'd escape the pain once and for all. However, I still had a subconscious fear that I would go to hell if I committed suicide. I tried researching the truth of this but could never come up with the answer. I'm glad at the time I didn't know the answer because I believe in some ways not knowing helped keep me alive.

After a couple of years into my adventure with bipolar disorder, I went to Ingrid's house one day wearing a washcloth on my wrist. I showed it to her while I was still bleeding. I assured her I'd call my therapist or psychiatrist, but I never did.

To make matters worse, I relapsed on alcohol whenever I'd cut my wrists. The numbing from the alcohol helped me withstand even more physical pain, allowing me to cut deeper. As I continued to go deeper, I started to feel excruciating pain. The combination of alcohol and self-injury was a risky, lethal combination.

I made it a habit to keep pills and razor blades in my purse in case I wanted to commit suicide. There were so many times when I'd go driving then stop in a parking lot and argue with myself:

"Should I do it?"

"No, I can't."

"Yes, I need to stop this pain. I should just do it. My kids would be better off without me. They don't need a mentally ill alcoholic mom for a mother."

Then there were times when I parked outside a hospital emergency room ready to slit my wrist and overdose on pills so that maybe someone would see me, and I wouldn't actually die. I wanted to live, yet I didn't. What I really wanted was to escape the continual living hell of my mind. But there was no way out.

In addition to using razor blades, I also began burning myself. Ironing clothes one day, the thought came to me, *You should burn yourself.* I didn't want to listen to it. I tried to drown it out, but it got louder and louder. Soon, I was obsessing over whether or not I should do it. As I slowly pushed the iron back and forth over the clothes, I became trapped in my own maniacal world. I didn't feel like I was present on earth at that moment, but rather only present in the world that existed in my mind.

I couldn't take the thought any longer, so I placed the iron directly on my arm. At first, it just felt like a little burn. Then it began to really hurt...a lot! I ran to the sink and poured cold water over it, but by then the damage was done. Even after I had cooled it off, the pain remained. But, strangely, I enjoyed it and delighted in seeing the scar it imprinted on my arm.

From that moment on, I continued to burn myself, and the burns got worse each time, leaving larger scars. I'd wear long-sleeved shirts to hide them, hoping to conceal my behavior from others. I couldn't afford to tell anyone that I was burning myself, or I'd definitely end up in the psych ward again.

Close Call

"There's nothing you need to be concerned about," I responded to my masseuse, trying to hide the fear in my voice. Due to the extreme stress in my life, I began having back pain. Back pain was common for me ever since I injured my lower back long jumping in college, but my current stress had intensified it. Even though I loved to inflict pain on myself through self-injury, I didn't want to live with back pain. I think it was that I wanted to control the pain. For years, everyone controlled me, and I didn't have a choice. I was trapped. But now, I wanted—needed—to control my world.

I started seeing a chiropractor to help with the pain, and he suggested getting deep-tissue massages. Although I was pretty good at hiding places where I self-injured, the masseuse wondered why I continually had wounds whenever I came to see her. She'd ask, "How did this happen?" and I'd lie to her every time.

Because of the pattern, she sensed something was wrong. She finally asked me if I was being abused by my husband. I told her no, but I feared that she'd say something that would get Claude or me in trouble. The moment she asked me about my wounds, I became anxious. I couldn't allow my secret out! There'd be so much shame if others besides my closest friends and support system knew about this.

I already had a difficult time with shame, and I'd frequently meet with my pastor and Ingrid to talk with them about it. I knew they were safe, and their house was a safe place. One day, as I was walking with my head down in shame, my pastor said to me, "Nichole, one day you'll be able to hold your head up high." I'll never forget that. His words spoke life to me in the moment. I believe God was trying to put hope back into me because He knew if any was left, it was a very thin thread.

As I nervously paid and left the chiropractor's office after my massage that day, I never went back. I was too afraid and full of shame to ever see this woman again. She knew I had a secret, even if she didn't know what it was. I was being found out. I'd have to be more careful in the future.

When I got home, I did what I often had to do. I went upstairs into my closet and cried my eyes out. I think I cried tears that I'd held in my whole life. I cried and screamed out to God, "Help me! I don't want to live anymore! Please help me, Lord! Help me to want to live for my family! Help me to be able to endure this pain."

I knew bipolar disorder was incurable, yet I'd still cry out, "Lord, please heal me. Have mercy on me, and heal me." In those moments, I'd always feel the Holy Spirit's comfort. It's as if He was cradling me in His arms of love. After weeping and letting it all out, I'd wipe the tears away and try to get on with life, even though life was very scary.

Afraid to Live and Afraid to Die

Around this time, along with self-harm, I began binge eating. I'd wake up in the morning to find wrappers in the kitchen for food that I didn't remember eating. I knew it had to be me who ate the food because no one else in my family would do this. Sometimes when I'd take my prescription medication for sleep, I'd become not only sleepy but also forgetful. Many times I'd fall asleep while bingeing on food.

When things had turned the worse for me, I was at my lowest weight. I was very skinny due to depression, but as I continued to go from one escape to the other, this time with food, I started to gradually gain weight. But, along with the weight came shame. At one point I was taking seven different medications, which also contributed to weight gain.

Gaining weight caused me to become even more self-conscious, which led to even greater self-hatred, if that was possible. I was becoming a completely different person, even on the outside. I didn't like who I was and who I was continuing to become. That person scared me. I couldn't even be alone with that person because I hated her so much.

Along with the weight gain came panic attacks. I didn't know what a panic attack was until I started seeing a psychiatrist. Apparently, I'd been having them for years, unaware of what they were. The attacks caused my heart to suddenly start racing uncontrollably. I'd have to lie down and calmly breathe in and out until they went away. They made me wonder if I was having a heart attack, which was quite frightening. The panic attacks reminded me of how out of control my life really was in many ways.

To me, it was much easier to think about suicide than to think about what a horrible person I was and how I kept failing God and everyone else. I simply couldn't do what the Bible said. I was a failure, and I knew in my heart God was mad at me. I just couldn't face Him. In many ways, I was afraid to live and afraid to die. I had thoughts of dying and seeing the Father and having Him judge me for every wrong in my life. I could imagine the look of disappointment on His face. How could I face him while living, and how could I face Him in death when He'd be able to talk to me about all of my failures?

I didn't know about God's love and goodness at this point. I didn't know that God is a good God. I saw Him as someone who'd bless me when I obeyed Him or punish me if I failed. After all, that's what happened in the Old Testament.

Each day, I'd open my AA devotional and read that day's devotion. I tried to pray to God to the best of my ability. Through shame and desperation, I'd plea with Him to give me the strength to make it "one day at a time." In AA, we'd talk about living life one moment and one day at a time. I'd think, *Well, if you add up one day at a time, it still means forever, and that means I can never drink again — whether it's one day at a time or not.*

I had a hard time with the concept of living in the moment. My mind always wanted to go to the future. As a child, I'd developed a fear of the future. I used to have to monitor my environment and plan my next move in order to survive, maintain peace, and not get into trouble. I learned quickly how *not* to live in and enjoy the moment. It was a habit for me to think negatively and to think the worst about my future.

"I Hate Me!"

It had been several years since my bipolar diagnosis. I tried desperately to calm the voices in my head that day, but yet again, nothing worked. I'm sure I'd called my psychiatrist to inform him I was having a hard time, and he most likely made a change in my medication. That was usually the case. He'd also ask me if I was suicidal, and oftentimes I'd lie and say no because I didn't want to go into the psych ward. I hated that place of darkness and turmoil, where I felt like a prisoner. I'd do anything to not have to go there.

But nothing was helping me on that particular day, so I decided to pull out my razor blade and describe what I was feeling on my body somewhere. I knew that I needed to hide it, so I used the blade to cut two-inch-block letters onto my stomach: "I HATE ME!"

After I had "written" on my stomach, it dawned on me that these words would leave a scar that would be forever etched on my body. I immediately started to feel shame and thought, *What have I done?* Often, in the moment of torment, I was so wrapped up in the thought of escape, that was all I could think about. But once I had relapsed or self-injured, immediately thoughts of shame and guilt flooded my mind. I called this the cycle of hell in my life: torment—suicidal thinking—get drunk—self-injury—shame and guilt—repeat.

I had absolutely no idea how to escape this thinking. After all, bipolar disorder was incurable, and it was normal for people with that disease to be suicidal. According to the Depression and Bipolar Support Alliance, bipolar disorder is the sixth leading cause of disability in the world, and one in five people affected by it commits suicide ("Bipolar Disorder Statistics," dbsalliance.org). I knew about these statistics and honestly didn't know how my story would end. Would I ever go through with it or not? I had no idea.

As I struggled with what I had done to my stomach, I started to feel the intense pain from the wounds, so I taped pieces of gauze over my belly. As I went about my day, getting ready for my weekly recovery support meeting that night, the physical pain of what I had done was nearly overwhelming. But I needed to be there for my kids when they arrived home from school. I knew that once Claude came home from work, I could then leave for my meeting.

Facing the Group

For the entire drive to my meeting, I wrestled with whether I should tell the group what I did. Each of them was a recovering alcoholic or drug addict, but none had a bipolar disorder. They didn't understand the extreme mental torment I was experiencing. In some ways, even though the group was a wonderful support system, they didn't really know how to truly help me. All of the regulars that attended had many years of sobriety, and I felt as though they started giving up hope on me. When I'd see others give up hope on me when I didn't even have hope for myself, it was very difficult. People could try to hide the hopelessness they felt for me, but I could see it in their eyes.

As I reluctantly walked into the group that night, I had no idea what would transpire. Even though I tried to remain quiet, someone called me out on the pain she saw on my face. She knew something was very wrong with me, but it didn't surprise her, as this pattern had been repeated with me time and time again.

I began explaining what I had done, and the group was extremely concerned. They all insisted that I get more help. They had compassion on me because they'd all been through some horrible trials in their lives as well. They understood pain. They understood trauma and addiction. Most of them even understood the shame of relapse. Those in my group came from all different backgrounds.

One was a wife of a well-respected heart surgeon. Others were rather wealthy, while others were just normal parents like me. If people were to view most of us only from our exterior, they wouldn't suspect that we were all recovering alcoholics and drug addicts. We never know what people have been through just by looking at them.

Leaving the meeting that night, I headed to my car and waited for one of the guys in the group who had parked next to me. As I saw him approach his car, I called out his name. When he came over, I started talking to him and decided to show him what I had done. I could tell it was hard for him to look at the wound. He was filled with shock, fear, and disgust. But it also seemed he had pity on me, wondering if I would make it. After he encouraged me to get more help, I felt ashamed again.

Now alone in my car, I was ready to drive home, but I was feeling depressed and anxious. On the way home, I had pictured myself crossing the center line on the highway so I could hit someone head-on and die. But I didn't want to hurt anyone else, so I knew that wasn't a viable option. I was comforted again by thinking that soon I'd be free forever from this hell on earth. Even though I was scared of God's judgment when I died, I knew that heaven was a wonderful place filled with joy and peace. I just wasn't sure if I'd make it there if I committed suicide.

Before heading to bed that night, I took some pain medicine along with the medication cocktail for bipolar disorder. If I didn't have the sleep medication, I would've been up half the night with mental anguish. Instead, I slept through the night and woke up to a new day. Unfortunately, the promise of a day of new beginnings quickly faded, as I instantly remembered that I was living a nightmare. I spent the day curled up in a ball on my couch, barely able to function.

Bible Studies and Vodka

One bright spot during this time was that my church had become my new, safe family. I could be vulnerable with a small group of women, which I considered a gift from God in many ways, even though I'd often regret sharing my heart. I was slowly learning to trust others and open up about what was going on inside. I continued therapy with a counselor who was like a mother figure to me. I began trusting her with my heart, and she'd help me to understand more of what was happening.

I continued attending Bible studies as much as possible. Deep down, I believed God would be happy if I did that, and it would please Him and earn me extra points with Him. I also felt that His Word would give me hope to continue living. Perhaps I'd find some peace. I knew that only God could help me with that because nothing else had ever worked.

Although I still attended Bible studies, the mania and depression continued, so I felt I needed to numb myself. I learned in AA that vodka was a strong drink with an odor that could be hidden. I went to the store and, making sure no one saw me, purchased a bottle. After my kids went to school, I had to get ready for Bible study. I was so tormented that morning that I decided to pour a large glass of vodka and orange juice. I put the glass in my car's cup holder and drove to Bible study.

I was risking getting pulled over by the police, but I'd only had a few sips while driving. I knew the small amount wouldn't affect my ability to drive by the time I went the couple of miles to Bible study. When I got to the Bible study, I downed the glass before heading in. I walked in with a fake smile on my face trying to hide my deep pain, shame, and hopelessness.

During worship, I began crying as I sensed the Holy Spirit comforting me and trying to provide much needed hope. As we started going through the questions in the Bible study, I raised my hand and asked if anyone knew whether a Christian who committed suicide would go to heaven. They all knew I was bipolar and an alcoholic. And, they understood that I was suicidal and had been in the psych ward. I'd often be on the prayer chain at church, so people knew I was a ticking time bomb emotionally. When I asked that question, some of the women figured that meant I was suicidal, and they had a look of concern.

I never did get an answer to my question that day, but at least no one smelled alcohol on my breath. In some ways, I'd hoped someone would. "Who will help me?" the little girl in me was desperately crying out. I knew, though, that no one really could. I had an incurable illness that affected my brain, and no one could fix my brain.

Trying to Be Normal

Life continued, and I tried my best to be a model mom to my kids. I'd throw outstanding birthday parties for them and take them to different activities or over to friends' houses. I'd try to take care of the house as much as possible, but it became increasingly harder, as my cycles got worse and worse. Before my life fell apart, my house was spotless. The laundry was always done, and I'd cook gourmet meals for my family. To go from perfectly managing a household to barely functioning was difficult to swallow.

I started buying alcohol and hiding it in the house, and I started taking myself to different restaurants in other towns where no one knew me. I'd order wine and bring my notebook to look like I was doing something important. I'd sip on wine and write furiously in the notebook. What people didn't know is that I was writing goodbye letters. I filled pages and pages of notebooks with goodbye letters.

One day, Claude and I were desperate for help, so a meeting was arranged for the elders of our church to come over and pray with me. It was on a day when I gave in to temptation and went to the basement to find the hidden wine bottles. I knew they were coming over, so I tried to pull myself together. I remember the elders talking with us and asking me if I had alcohol that day. I admitted that I had. Claude was so disappointed. They honestly didn't know what to do with me.

They prayed the best prayer that they knew how, but no one ever prayed for my healing. After all, bipolar was incurable. Also, they believed that God sometimes chooses not to heal people for certain reasons, so why bother praying for healing?

I figured God didn't want to heal me because I kept messing up all the time, and I was nothing more than an alcoholic, mentally ill mother who couldn't get my life together. I felt like the black sheep of the church, even though it was a safe place for me. I knew God was my only hope of making it in life, even if I did fear Him at times.

Because of my incurable illness, Claude and I decided to take action and get the help we needed to create the most normal life we could for our family. The house was becoming a disaster and it was hard for me to function, so we hired a college-aged girl to help with various household chores. I was so grateful she was there, but at times I resented her taking up space in my home. Seeing her reminded me that I was so crazy that I couldn't even manage my own house. It angered me that I was that sick in my mind. I was a stay-at-home mom with time on my hands, and I couldn't even function enough to do the laundry!

I was ashamed that I needed help because I was used to doing everything myself. Growing up, I didn't get much help with anything. I had to figure out my homework by myself, along with most other things because no one was emotionally available. Having someone in my house helping me, when I've always kept my house immaculate was very humbling. I tried to stay out of the girl's way as much as possible, but when I was really distressed, I'd send her home early so I could self-injure and relapse on alcohol. I wanted to be back to functioning before my kids came home from school. I'd do whatever I could to appear "normal."

CHAPTER 10

FROM HOPE TO DESPAIR

As I continued to see my therapist, she began noticing how much discernment and wisdom I had concerning people. Growing up, I had to analyze everyone's next move, which forced me to closely observe those around me. During the course of the many conversations that my therapist and I had in my moments of peace and clarity, she recognized this gift of discernment and began to encourage me in it.

Whenever God used someone to speak life into me, it was a gift and a blessing that little by little helped chisel away my negative heart messages. The therapist suggested that I go to college to become a certified addiction counselor. Her feedback, combined with similar positive feedback from other therapists in the various rehab programs I was in, convinced me to enroll in a local community college. I've always loved learning and did well in college when I attended earlier in my life. Strangely enough, I enjoyed the challenge of writing papers and taking tests!

Right now, I needed to focus on something other than my problems. I needed a positive distraction. I enrolled in psychology classes, as well as a class on addictions. I attended college a couple of times a week, and I finally started to feel normal. No one knew me, and no one knew my secrets of having a bipolar disorder and being a recovering alcoholic. I was able to fit in.

I got all A's my first semester by working hard and throwing myself into my studies. I finally had some hope for my future and felt like I could use my pain to help others in their journey. Although I was still fearful of my own future, this newfound hope kept me going. I had a purpose.

At one point, my class was required to record a mock therapy session on a tape recorder and play it in front of everyone. We were to write everything out that would be said between a therapist and a patient. I used a scenario from my own life, and my fictional male patient was bipolar and a self-injurer. I received an A on the assignment. It was an easy A, as this scenario was such a huge part of what I was living. I figured I may as well use all the therapy I was receiving to my advantage.

When the second semester started, I was eager to take an extra class to finish sooner, but Claude was not in agreement. I still had a house to take care of; counseling, AA, and psychiatrist appointments to attend; Bible studies to go to; and other responsibilities. I had a lot going on, and Claude was afraid I would soon become overwhelmed. There was always a fear in the back of everyone's mind that I would relapse again. My life was such a roller coaster, and no one knew when I might crash—including me.

After several arguments with him, I agreed to take fewer classes. I didn't want to face the reality that I was limited in life because of illness. Even though I reluctantly took fewer classes, I still felt motivated that I could do more. I pictured myself counseling people and helping them—telling them that I could understand their pain and their addiction. I was encouraged that I could be a counselor who had gone through the same trials my future clients were going through.

The Voices Return

I enjoyed going to school a couple of days a week then spending time at the library doing homework. I loved feeling like a normal student. I believed I was accomplishing something worthwhile for a change. After a while, however, the negative voices returned and started to slowly drag me downhill. While in my addiction class one night, I listened to the professor talk about addiction while I told myself, "I am not an alcoholic." I looked in the textbook that described addictions while listening to the tormenting voices telling me, "You are not an alcoholic. Who cares what everyone says? You can drink normally."

From that moment on, I started to unravel. The following week before class, I stopped at a restaurant, ordered a beer, and got out my notebook. I began writing goodbye letters again, as I drank my beer and looked around to make sure no one saw me. It was as if I had a double life. That night, I went to class and decided even more that I was definitely not an alcoholic. I started to get angry at everyone around me and at myself. I was ashamed for relapsing again and disappointing everyone. I knew people would eventually find out because it was impossible for me to keep it a secret.

The torment continued into the next day. I decided to completely give in to it and buy a bottle of wine and drink it while slitting my wrist. As I was cutting myself with loud music blaring in the background, I noticed that I'd cut deeper than I ever had before. The bleeding was intense. It was always a relaxing feeling when I'd watch the blood flow, but this time I was actually concerned. I stopped cutting and attempted to stop the bleeding. After soaking many gauze pads in blood, the bleeding finally ceased.

I bandaged my wrist and realized I had to hide it from everyone, especially Claude. He'd know immediately when he saw it. He was always afraid to leave me alone, and I understood why. I was even more fearful than he was of what I would do while he was gone. We had a support system in place that either of us could call at anytime, but there was still a lot of anxiety within both of us. I made it through the episode without him noticing, but the next morning the bleeding began again when I was taking a shower. This time it wouldn't stop.

I got out of the shower and frantically dressed, trying not to get blood everywhere. I kept putting gauze pads on my wrist while I got my kids ready for school. Eventually, I ran out of gauze and bandages and had to call my neighbor, Melissa. She asked to see my wrists, and she was quite concerned when I showed her. Not surprisingly, she didn't believe my story of me getting cut while I was making a meal for the Crockpot. She immediately called Claude and told him to meet us at the ER.

ER Visit

I'm sure Claude was both worried and frustrated when he received my neighbor's call to go to the hospital. He'd already missed many days of work due to my sicknesses. He held a very high position in his company, and without his coworkers knowing what was going on with me, it became difficult for him. I knew he had a right to divorce me because I wasn't the woman he'd married. I had caused so many problems for our family, which was the last thing I wanted to do. I grieved at the pain I had caused everyone. This is why I often listened to the voices telling me that my family would be better off without me, and I should just commit suicide and get it over with.

When I arrived at the ER, I had to tell them why I was there, and I admitted that I cut myself. It was so humiliating and shameful to say that I did this to myself. I saw the look of disgust the nurse had on her face, and I knew then I wouldn't be treated as a normal patient. They'd view me as a crazy person. Deep down, I knew there was something really wrong with me, but I didn't know how to fix it. I didn't know how to be well.

When I sat down, I noticed that blood was dripping onto the floor. I went back to the nurse and told her I needed new bandages. She looked annoyed but also concerned. They got me in faster to see a doctor due to the blood continuing to flow from my wrist. When the doctor came in to see me, I had to again explain what I had done, and I became petrified that they would send me back to the psych ward. I definitely did not want to go to the psych ward! Plus, I was finally doing something I wanted to do by going to college, and I didn't want to miss my classes.

The doctor asked me for my psychiatrist's name so he could call. I convinced him I was doing okay and would see my therapist right away. I breathed a sigh of relief when I knew I had talked him out of sending me to the psych ward. He said I'd need stitches in my wrist to stop the bleeding, and then proceeded to stitch me up. After doing so, his face turned serious, and with a look of grave concern, he stared straight into my eyes and said, "If you continue to cut your wrists like this, one day you'll be successful. You need to stop doing this now," and emphasized "now."

He knew I was a potential suicide waiting to happen. When he said those words, part of me became fearful, but another part felt excited. I experienced happiness thinking of the day when hell on earth would finally come to an end.

Claude met me at the ER, and we went home together. I'm sure he was wondering how he could ever rescue his wife and keep her from not harming herself. But I didn't even know that answer myself.

Dumpster Diving

All I knew to do was to continue going to my AA meetings, counseling, psychiatric sessions, and Bible study, and continue taking my many medications that frequently changed. As time went on, I thought of new ways to self-destruct. I started taking the sleeping pill Ambien during the day to escape. I'd break it in half and use it to alter my mind. It shouldn't be taken during the day, and I knew it, but I was always looking for new ways to escape.

I also began researching how sniffing various chemicals would affect me. I went into my garage and began experimenting with this.

At one point, I was scared that I'd overdose on pills, so I threw away the medications that my doctor gave me to help with extreme anxiety. In an effort to fight the temptation to overdose on them, I thought it would be best if they were in the garbage. I'd also thrown away some alcohol that was still in the house. I tried to fight relapsing again and not killing myself. I knew the way to fight at that moment was to rid myself of all temptations. As soon as I threw everything away, the battle ensued between keeping everything in the garbage and getting it out. Once again, the voices of addiction and self-destruction won the day.

I marched outside and began digging through my trashcan. It was garbage day, and the trash truck would soon be coming to collect the garbage. It was now or never. I thought about how horrified I would be if my neighbors saw me. I knew it would only exacerbate the gossip that was going around about me, but the thought of getting rid of the pills and the alcohol was much worse to me at that moment than the consequences of getting caught.

My fears came to pass. My neighbor drove by my house and watched momentarily as I dug through my trash. But I didn't care. I was desperate! *Which bag did I put the pill bottles in?* After getting dirty and combing through several bags, I finally found what I was looking for and brought them inside. I gathered the pills and the bottle of wine and placed them all within reach. I don't remember what happened after that.

I Would Never Do That!

I do, however, specifically remember the humiliation of being seen digging through the garbage, desperate to get my escapes back. That is what addiction does. The voice of addiction continually cries out to its victims, telling them they can't live without whatever their addiction is. It tells them to do stupid and crazy things in order to escape. The voice of addiction screams at its victims until they give in and feel temporary peace. But when that peace wears off, the voice screams louder and louder. Unfortunately, many people don't make it; many die in their addiction.

I completely understand why some don't make it. When all the alcohol was out of the house and my torment continued, I'd do anything to find a way to escape. I'd heard many stories from being in AA and the psych ward — stories where I'd say to myself, *Wow! That's really bad! I'd never do that.* Well, here I was now doing some of the same things I vowed I'd never do.

For instance, I'd heard of people relapsing on mouthwash and vanilla extract. I said I'd never do that, but I did. I remember the mouthwash calling my name one night, and I couldn't resist. I took a gulp, and it was disgusting. Yet, I knew one sip would do nothing. I decided to down a lot of it so I could at least use it as an escape. When I would do something like this, there was always a part of me that thought, *I'm really not well in the head. I must be sick. What person in their right mind would ever do something like this? I'm a mother and a Christian. How could I stoop so low?* But addiction causes people to become someone they never thought they'd ever be and to do things they never thought they'd ever do.

In addition to the mouthwash, I purchased a few bottles of vanilla extract in order to get a buzz. After taking several sips, I couldn't continue. I found it nauseating, and after drinking it, I felt even more repulsed with myself. Although the vanilla extract didn't work, I continued to take increasingly more risks with my life. In addition to all the other ways I attempted to harm myself, I started trying to break my bones or break my neck in a way that wouldn't look like a suicide attempt.

I began throwing myself down the stairs to cause a broken neck or paralysis injury. I figured if I was paralyzed, at least I'd be safe. This method of harming myself was very scary. Even in times of torment, I decided after several attempts at doing this that I'd prefer to die in a different way or to feel the pain of a razor blade. I inflicted many rug burns, bruises, and scrapes, but then decided I'd had enough. At this point in my life, the talons of bondage and self-destruction had penetrated so deeply, there wasn't much I wouldn't try in order to escape and get some relief.

CHAPTER 11

ENCOUNTER WITH THE FATHER

I couldn't control the weeping in the moment, unable to believe what I just heard. Could it be true? Is God that good? I didn't know at the time. I started to calm down after a moment of crying, knowing that I had heard my heavenly Father's voice. Even though I wasn't experienced at hearing His voice speaking to me — or so I thought — I knew without a shadow of a doubt that He had just spoken to my heart. He pursued me with His love. He was never giving up on me.

After a morning of another mixed episode of mania and depression, I did what was common for me to do. I was upstairs in my room with the door closed. No one was home. I never self-injured when the kids were home, as I tried to the best of my ability to hide everything from them. But on this day, something different happened. I had just cut my arm with a razor blade and was watching the blood flow, when all of a sudden, I heard a voice clearly and lovingly say to me, "You don't have to do that anymore because My Son shed His blood for you." I knew instantly that the voice was that of Father God.

This was an encounter with the Lord — a love encounter that happened in the middle of my bondage — that I will never forget it. My first thought was, *Why is God talking to me when I'm clearly sinning in this moment?* I had believed that God would only be interested in a relationship with me when I got my act together. I figured that as soon as I was able to stop relapsing on alcohol and self-injury and stop entertaining suicidal thoughts, maybe then God would want fellowship with me. I thought that He would require me to remove all the sin from my life before He would love me, bless me, or possibly heal me.

This encounter with Him began to revolutionize my theology, but I still had a long way to go. I cried after I heard His voice, realizing that He touched my heart deeply with His love and grace in the midst of my darkest pain. He knew exactly what to say to me. I had His full attention!

Of course, we all have His full attention at every moment, but it was as if His heart could no longer take the pain that I was enduring, and He knew He needed to do something drastic to get me to stop believing the lies about Him. What a loving Father we have!

I kept my encounter with the Lord in my mind as much as I could. And, as time went on, I tried to accept the fact that I was bipolar, and it was incurable. I truly believed that I would have this label for the rest of my life. It was my identity now. When people who knew me saw me, I knew that was one of the first things on their mind. To them, I was the "unstable, not in her right mind, bipolar one." Because I lived life through the lens of rejection my whole life, I was sure they would eventually reject me, which caused me to believe that I was never completely accepted or safe. It didn't matter how much love was poured onto me, in the back of my mind, I couldn't fully receive it. I wanted to receive it, but it just seemed too good to be true. My reasoning was, if I received their love and they rejected me, it would be too painful to deal with.

In order to accept the disease, I did a lot of research. I ordered every book there was on bipolar disorder. I even subscribed to a bipolar magazine specifically for people living with the disease. I finally felt like I belonged somewhere. I decided in my heart that I would embrace this illness, and I would be proud to wear the badge of bipolar disorder. I knew I could advocate for others suffering from it. I could announce to them that we aren't abnormal. We can't help that our brains were formed differently. I could help others believe that we aren't crazy!

An opportunity where I could share my experiences, educate people on living with bipolar, and share Jesus all at the same time, soon presented itself at my church. I had been highly involved in various areas of my church, and I even had the idea of starting a coffee café after the services. I was excited when the leadership asked me to research industrial coffee makers and also to organize and start the café. I was creative and knew that I needed to use my mind for positive endeavors. When I was involved in creative projects, it helped distract me from my problems and helped me feel "normal."

I had a professional coffee maker at home and grew to love making different-flavored cappuccinos and lattes for my friends. I was excited to use my coffee knowledge and giftedness to volunteer at church, bringing some fun and fellowship after the services.

Wrong Thinking

In addition to running the church café and being involved in Bible studies and family home groups, I was invited to speak at a women's conference where I was asked to talk about living with bipolar disorder. The invitation was an honor to me. At the conference, I sat in a circle with the women and shared about bipolar disorder being the "thorn in my flesh," referencing the apostle Paul in the Bible and his thorn in the flesh (2 Corinthians 12:7). I didn't have the true revelation of this scripture at the time, so I incorrectly stated that God gave me this disease, yet I still gave Him glory for it. I also shared how He would help me live with it.

Somehow, after sharing all of this, I didn't feel uplifted. Who would? Who would be encouraged knowing that God gave him or her a mind-tormenting disease that caused suicidal thinking and severe depression? Who would feel uplifted thinking that he or she has an incurable disease and can barely function at times, and all the while God demands glory and praise in the midst of it?

It was hard for me to praise God for being bipolar. But, out of fear of going to hell or punishment, I gave Him glory for it. I became fearful when I read about what happened to people in the Bible who disobeyed God. I had determined that if I was going to die, it would be by my hands, not God's.

What I didn't realize at the time is that the Father's desire is for us to experience His amazing love so we can heal and receive the love of others. At this point in my life, I couldn't receive God's love for me. I hated myself, and as a result, I couldn't receive the love of others either. The smallest thing could set me off, like the cancelation of a coffee date. It was a terrible way to live. For me, the cancelation of plans meant that the other person didn't care for me and that I was being rejected. I couldn't see situations through a normal lens. I viewed everything through the skewed lens of rejection.

Additionally, the negative childhood messages I had written on my heart had continued into my adulthood and my relationships. These messages brought failure and defeat and caused extreme fear and anxiety. Living with core beliefs, such as: no one loves me, I'm defective, I'm unworthy, I don't deserve love, and everyone will ultimately leave me, was a torturous way to live life.

Our lives are the result of what we believe about ourselves. Right believing leads to right living. My core beliefs were frustrating for those around me, including my own husband. He couldn't understand how I could still think that people were rejecting me when everyone was still around. All the people I feared would leave me never left. In fact, they're still in my life to this day!

Yet, I'd subconsciously test them at times to see if they'd really stay. For me, it was too good to be true. Today, I'm saddened for the little girl in me who was abandoned and abused. I understand now why she grew up not trusting people. I understand why she grew up afraid to receive love from others.

One-Star Motel

A good example of how my negative core beliefs affected me during this time occurred at a counseling meeting I attended due to another relapse. Claude and I had an appointment together to see my counselor, Judy, and during the meeting, I became visibly upset. Judy was showing me tough love, and I had perceived it as rejection. During the session, she kicked me out of the meeting, and I was ordered to go to the waiting room. I sat there in stark fear, not knowing what she and Claude would do with me. I felt like a little child, where Claude was my parent. I wondered how he might punish me. I knew that Judy could be tough at times, and I had no idea what Claude was going to say.

I soon found out as he stormed out of Judy's office. "I'm taking you home and taking you somewhere," he said angrily. I got scared immediately. As we approached our car, he told me he was taking me to a motel to live for a week. I would be given some cash to be used only for food. I would have no car and no phone. He said in a voice that was out of character for him, "This is so you can see what your life will be like if you continue drinking."

I knew Judy had influenced Claude in this decision. I knew my husband didn't want to do this, but he didn't know what else to do. But I also knew that he would listen to Judy and have to follow through on her instructions. Immediately, I began thinking, *I'm bad. I'm defective. They want to kick me out. I'm loved only conditionally. I'm loved when I act right, but when I mess up, people leave me. I know deep down, I'll never be able to get my act together, so people will leave me and I'll be all alone.*

I tried arguing with Claude on the way home, but he wouldn't give in. I reluctantly packed my bag, and we headed to a very inexpensive, run-down motel room. He picked that motel on purpose to show me what my life would be like if I chose alcohol over my family. I didn't want to choose alcohol or mental illness over my family or anything else. I was trying everything I knew to do to be well, but I couldn't get rid of the mental torment.

Since bipolar was incurable, that meant a lifetime of ups and downs. What hope could I have if I was doing everything I was told, but my willpower wasn't working? I had no idea how I was going to make it. In some ways, I felt as though I was being punished for being mentally ill. I grew up fearing punishment, and when it came to pass in my life, it was devastating. It resurfaced the anxiety I experienced in my childhood, including the deep fear of abandonment and rejection.

I discovered that I was more angry at myself than anyone. I began asking myself, "Why can't I get it right? Why am I such a failure?" Being a failure was another core belief I had. The only way I thought I could fix that in my mind was to be perfect all the time, which I knew was impossible. I didn't know how to give myself grace. I didn't know how to love myself. That night when Claude took me to the motel, I packed my Bible with my clothes, hoping I would find something positive to hold on to. I knew deep down that God was my only hope.

Claude came into the lobby with me and checked me in. He took me to my tiny room where I had only basic necessities like a bed and a shower and a lamp. The motel was run down with a horrible musty odor, and the people there were scary. I was fearful to be left alone there, but I knew I had no choice. Claude gave me a certain amount of cash, saying, "You can either use this for food or alcohol; it's your choice."

His words and tone saddened me. It wasn't the real Claude speaking to me. I knew he'd been influenced by Judy and possibly others. I was certain that everyone would be talking about me, and it would all be negative. I was convinced that everyone thought I was a loser. Everyone would think I didn't care and that I wasn't trying hard enough.

When Claude left me alone in that dark room, away from my family, with no car and no phone, I started weeping. I cried out to the Lord in desperation. "Lord, why aren't You helping me? I need Your help! I can't live without You. I can't do this on my own. I don't know what I'm doing wrong! I don't know why I keep failing. Lord, I need answers. I need You to help me…please!"

I sobbed for hours on the bed, not knowing what to do. Eventually, I left the room and walked around, searching for food. I saw a liquor store across the street and was tempted to buy alcohol to numb myself, but I quickly shut down those thoughts because I didn't want to lose my family. Instead, I bought a hamburger and fries from Steak-N-Shake and returned to my room.

No Magic Wand

The following day, I called a woman I knew in AA. She offered to take me to meetings, and I asked her to become my new sponsor.

When she agreed, I felt as though I had something—someone—to help me through, since I believed I had been abandoned by my family and friends.

I was an active participant at the meetings—thrilled to be going and feeling like I belonged. Since I was excited about it, I told my family and friends how I found someone to take me, and they were actually upset about this. I was shocked! They said they wanted me to be completely alone and isolated so I could think about my situation. What they didn't understand was that isolated thinking is what got me into trouble in the first place.

Once again, I felt like a failure. I had believed the AA meetings were the right thing to do at the time, but everyone else saw it differently. At the end of the week, I was proud that I had money left over. I gave it back to Claude to show him that I didn't spend it on alcohol. I told myself, "I'll never relapse again. This was my bottom." The motel experience was a definite low in my life. I felt ashamed for having to go that low, and being a mother only magnified it.

The last thing I wanted to do was cause my children pain; they were my life. I tried desperately to be well for them, but honestly, I didn't know how. I wanted a magic wand that I could wave and make everything all better, but I knew I'd never get one. No one gets a magic wand in this life.

The week I came home, I made an appointment with my psychiatrist. He was infuriated that Judy influenced Claude to put me in a motel. That was confusing to me, as I had been trying to accept what was done as an act of love, but his reaction caused me to believe it was an act of injustice and punishment instead. Thinking about what he said made me mistrust my therapist from that point on. I believed that Judy was yet another person who abandoned and rejected me.

I realize that when Claude talked with our support group, it was all done in love, as well as concern for my well-being. No one knew what to do with me. I was a new case for everyone! I didn't even know what was right for me. But deep down, I don't believe that tough love is the right approach for everyone, especially for those who suffer with a debilitating fear of abandonment. Instead, we need for people to speak words of life and love to us.

I needed a constant reminder from those in my life—especially in times of failure—that they loved me and believed in me. If someone had said to me, "Nichole, we love you. We know you're better than this. We know you can do all things through Christ who strengthens you. You're not acting like who you really are in Christ right now. Let me tell you the lies you're believing so you can counter them with the truth," this approach would've helped me so much more than isolating me in a motel.

CHAPTER 12

ANOTHER PROGRAM

Dr. Brown, my psychiatrist, was a loving Christian man and a gift from God at this time in my life. Throughout my journey, God had placed the right people across my path at just the right times. He had surrounded me with wonderful people as He tried to set me free from the belief that people didn't love me. He wanted me to trust again.

When I saw my psychiatrist on this particular day, I expressed to him that I was feeling suicidal again. He was a safe place for me. There were times I confided true feelings to him more than anyone else. I told him how desperately I wanted to cut myself and drink myself into oblivion and end my life. I knew that saying such things risked that I would be put back in the psych ward, but I also knew I needed help and needed to tell on myself. I guess I was hoping someone would say, "No, you'll never kill yourself. You'll be okay. You'll get to the other side of this."

But, the truth is, no one knew—including myself—if I would make it to the other side or not. People just hoped for the best, as did I. As time went on, I didn't know how much more bondage I could take. I was growing weary and so was everyone else in my life. I could see it on their faces, even when they tried hard to hide it.

When Dr. Brown heard how I was feeling, he decided to make a change in my medications and asked if I would be willing to go to an outpatient program for a few weeks. I agreed, thinking, *What did I have to lose?* It would mean going to the hospital day program for eight hours a day for intense therapy and group sessions again. I was excited thinking that I may see Elizabeth, my former counselor.

Art Class Anger

Organizing my household with three young children was difficult. Mom was going to be gone, yet again. How do you explain to kids that you're mentally sick? Most people have compassion on those who have a physical illness, but if someone is labeled "mentally ill," that person doesn't always receive the same compassion, as the person is viewed as an outcast. I've personally experienced this many times. I know now that a person who is mentally ill has likely experienced some form of trauma or abuse that has not been dealt with. I have compassion on those hurting, wounded people.

Our family pulled our schedule together, and I began the outpatient program the following day. I was determined that this time would be different. I had been through so many of these programs, I had lost hope that they could offer me anything positive. I believed that the peace I'd experience when I got through the program would eventually leave me. The main reason I wanted to try again was because I wasn't only suicidal, but I had relapsed again on alcohol and self-injury.

As I left for my first day, I did something I never thought I'd do. Feeling depressed and hopeless, I hid an open bottle of vodka in my car. Entering the hospital parking lot that morning, memories from previous visits flooded my mind. Before I went in, I decided to drink some of the vodka. Whenever I'd drink, my self-hatred increased. A sip of alcohol meant failure. It meant my life was out of control.

As I walked into the hospital, I had hoped to get Elizabeth for my therapist, but I learned that she had started working with the youth program, and I would be given someone else. I had finally trusted someone, and I wanted to continue building that trust, but I had no choice but to accept my new therapist. I was thrilled, however, when I discovered that I'd be with the same psychiatrist, Dr. Thomas, as before—also a caring, loving Christian like Dr. Brown. I knew that he understood us "bipolar people." He didn't judge me but tried to help me.

In my art therapy class that day, I had become agitated and depressed. I kept asking, "When is lunchtime?" The woman running the class was quite annoyed with me. In class, she asked us to draw a picture that represented our family using fairy tales. I drew a picture from *Cinderella*. I hated my stepmother, Mary. She stole my dad away from me. She controlled and ruined my family. My mother told her children that Mary stole my dad away from her, and I believed it. I hated Mary, and those feelings came through in my drawing.

Reliving childhood memories caused much pain that day, and I couldn't control my anger and rage. When it was my turn to describe what I drew, the pain was excruciating. A girl in the class shared about pain she felt concerning her father, and that caused more painful memories of my dad to arise. I didn't know what to do with these mixed emotions that were swirling in my head. I didn't know how to cope with the anguish. Then I had a thought.

There was a bar one block from the hospital. I decided I needed to get there quickly. I had to have a drink. This is why I kept asking, "When is lunch? When can we leave?" As soon as we had permission to go, I bolted from the hospital on my mission. I couldn't take the surge of emotions any longer. I couldn't deal with life. I had to escape.

A Lethal Combination

I'd been trying to do what everyone told me, but no one in my circle knew what it was like to live with bipolar disorder. No one knew what it was like to live with a tormented mind and not be able to escape that mind. After all, my mind was attached to me — I couldn't leave it behind! I was stuck with it, and I didn't know how to make it function properly. I wanted peace, and I wanted it now! The only way I knew how to get that peace was by drinking.

I sat on a barstool thinking how I hoped I wouldn't see anyone there I knew. I then proceeded to take some of my anti-anxiety medicine in order to jumpstart my escape. I ended up taking way more than I was supposed to and had a glass of wine to wash it down. I ordered some food for appearance's sake, but I had no intention of eating. As soon as the wine came, I gulped it down and ordered another.

At one point, I called a friend from church and told on myself. I told her what I was doing but asked her not to tell anyone. I was supposed to have a party at my house that night for another friend, and many of the ladies from church were coming. The person I called was also invited to the party, and even though I asked her not to, she called my other friends to tell them what was happening.

My lunch break was over and it was time to head back to the hospital and finish my program for the day. When I returned, I tracked down Elizabeth and told her what I did. She encouraged me to tell the group during my therapy session, which I was used to, as I frequently had to tell on myself during my AA meetings. Failure was more and more becoming my identity, along with the usual shame.

As my group sat in a circle, I stared blankly at the floor and confessed what I did over lunch. Someone took my anti-anxiety pills away and called Claude and Dr. Brown. They were debating putting me in the psych ward again, but I got on the phone and convinced both of them that I'd be okay and would finish the program.

The rest of the day was a complete blur. Elizabeth later told me that the hospital gave me a breathalyzer test to see if I could drive home. The breathalyzer indicated that I was sober, but I was definitely high on the medication. I don't have any recollection of taking the breathalyzer, but upon leaving, I do remember getting into my car and finding my bottle of vodka. As I gulped it down, I realized how truly out of control my life was.

On the way home, I somehow remembered that I was having a party at my house. Apparently, I stopped to buy snacks and drinks, although I don't remember doing so. Afterward, the horror of wondering how I acted and who may've seen me haunted me! But, the worst was yet to come.

Heading home, I was driving on a three-lane busy road by my house. By the grace of God, I was in the left lane. On three occasions, I started blacking out while driving, and each time the wheel rammed the curb, which startled me back awake. Had I been in the middle or the right lane, I no doubt would've hit other cars and could have either killed myself or someone else. I know I couldn't have lived with myself if I killed someone due to my intoxication. It would've been too much for me to bear. I praise God that He protected me and others, even in the midst of my mess.

Once I arrived home, I barely remembered the night. A couple of my friends came over to yell at me because they knew I was drunk, and they wanted to tell me they weren't coming to the party. As the time for the party drew near, some people called to ask for directions, and I didn't know how to tell them to get to my house, even though they lived close by. This was a clue to everyone that I had relapsed yet again.

When my guests started showing up, I tried hard to look sober, but it didn't work. Everyone knew what happened. Amazingly, they stayed and loved on me anyway. When I awoke the next morning, the horror of what I had done hit me. I humiliated myself yet again and let everyone down. How could I possibly make this up to my friends? I decided I needed to personally apologize to everyone who came to my party. I did, and they all graciously accepted my apology. Yet, I knew they still thought I was crazy.

Would I Ever Change?

How could anyone trust me with anything? I kept wondering over and over. I knew that I had to get dressed to go to the outpatient program despite how I felt. I somehow managed to dress, even though my body could barely move. I turned on worship music in my car and sobbed all the way to the hospital, repenting to the Lord the whole time. I asked God to somehow forgive me for failing Him yet again. I had hoped He would agree, but I wasn't sure He would. Maybe He thought I wasn't sorry enough. I was determined to show Him that I loved Him by not relapsing ever again. I would win His love back, I decided.

I parked my car and headed into the hospital, once again hanging my head, feeling hopeless and tired. The good news was that at least I had a place to process what I was going through. Nothing surprised anyone in those groups. There were bipolar people, depressed people, and schizophrenics. An inside joke was that none of the bipolar people in the group could sit still. We'd always be the ones fidgeting and moving around with anxiety. We understood each other. We understood the living hell we were all going through. And, we understood the shame we felt when people viewed us as defective and crazy.

One day while at the program, I wore bold-colored striped pants. Dr. Brown said to me, "Those are your bipolar pants!" We both had a good laugh. I had once learned that Van Gogh, along with some other well-known creative people, was possibly bipolar. I loved to paint, and I loved bold colors. Others often called me an artist, as I'd paint squares, diamonds, and stripes on walls for myself and even occasionally for others. I embraced that artistic side of the bipolar disorder. To me, this was a positive aspect of the disease, and because most of it was negative, I'd take anything positive associated with it that I could find.

After attending the outpatient program for a while and going to a psychiatrist, therapist, group therapy, and AA meetings that were held there, I finished the program and left. My treatment there allowed me to process a lot from my past, but it also further engrained to me that what I was dealing with was incurable. I left thinking that I'd probably have to be in and out of such programs the rest of my life.

I had heard some horrible stories while I was in the groups. The tormenting cycles I had were progressively getting worse, and I feared I'd end up like some of those I had met in my programs who were barely functioning. I left the hospital knowing I'd have to continue seeing my counselor and psychiatrist and continue going to AA meetings and addiction support groups.

I longed to return to my life of a stay-at-home mom where I didn't need all of these things. How did all of this happen? How did I get where I was? I knew that the childhood trauma I had endured took a toll on me and my brain. All the pain that I shoved inside for years kept gushing out, and I was still learning how to escape it. I had glimpses of crying out to God and letting Him comfort me and heal my broken heart, but I still had periods of self-injury and alcohol abuse.

I was learning how to live life like an adult, like everyone else. Healthy, trustworthy relationships were being modeled for me for the first time in my life, and I was learning how to be in relationships with others. It was painfully beautiful and scary all at once. I thank God that He surrounded me with wonderful people who loved me with the love of Christ.

The people He gave me continually interceded for my life. They saw my heart and saw the "real" me. In the temporary periods of calm, they saw that I was funny and caring and loving. They knew I was loyal and smart. They also knew that when the cycles started, they were no longer talking to the "real" Nichole. I had heard many times that I became a completely different person during my episodes, almost as if I was possessed. My voice even changed. My good friends knew right away, as soon as I'd answer the phone, whether I was in a good place or not. My husband said the same thing, and I know that the person I became frightened him.

CHAPTER 13

THE ROLLER COASTER RIDE CONTINUES

Based on my high school athleticism, Claude encouraged me to sign up for a mini-triathlon that was being held in our city. I was motivated when I registered, but as usual, my enthusiasm waned over time. To train, I began bike riding and going on short runs. I was told in all of my therapy programs that exercise would help me by increasing the healthy chemicals in my brain. I was willing to try anything and always loved a challenge!

In high school, I had been voted best female athlete my senior year, so I figured I could at least finish a mini-triathlon. It was a half-mile swim, a fourteen-mile bike ride, and a three-mile run. Swimming came easily to me, so I didn't practice much for that.

When I embarked on my training, cycles of mania and depression became evident again. At one point, I was in my psychiatrist's office with Claude, trying to talk them both out of me going through with the triathlon. I told them I wasn't ready, and I couldn't do it. I had no faith in myself, especially during times of depression. But neither budged in their belief that it would be good for me to do. I was angry about it at the time, but I reluctantly agreed that I'd follow through.

The day of the race, nervousness and excitement held a boxing match within my emotions. I arrived with Claude and some friends and checked in. At the start line for the half-mile swim, for some reason I became anxious about not wanting to do that part of the race. But, the whistle blew, and without another thought, I dove into the water. I began passing other swimmers, which made me feel good about myself. The field of swimmers was so large, I kept bumping into people and having some practically swim on top of me. Still, I kept telling myself, "You can do it! You can do it! Keep going."

This race was such a parallel for my life, as I needed to keep going no matter what obstacles I encountered. I emerged from the water tired but excited to have finished the first third of the race. Claude shouted at me, "Great job, Nichole!" That was all I needed to hear to keep going. I wanted to make him proud again. I knew he was proud to marry me, an American, back in the day. I was a cute, outgoing, funny American, and Claude was so happy to call me his wife.

Recently, however, I believed I had failed as a wife, and I had gained a fair amount of weight on top of everything else. I was no longer a "cute" American. I was a bipolar, overweight wife, who had to leave the family to go to programs just to survive and function. Life was so different now, so to hear Claude tell me, "Great job!" I knew I had to finish that race.

I ran and found my bike and completed the biking portion without a problem. I heard Claude cheering me on again, and then I made it to the start line of the road race. Running at this point was difficult, so I alternated running and walking. I didn't care; I just wanted to finish. After everything I'd gone through over the last five years, I knew I needed to make myself proud and press on to win that medal at the end.

I'll never forget looking past the finish line and seeing a big smile on Claude's face. He was so incredibly happy to see me cross that line. He immediately ran to me and threw his arms around me, telling me how proud he was of me. It felt so good to finish a triathlon. It was a huge accomplishment for me, which gave me much needed hope for my future.

As Claude and I talked later that evening, he told me, "You should write a book. You should write about living with bipolar disorder." He thought it would be amazing to share with others what I had learned with all I'd been through.

He also thought it was a good idea to have his mother come from France every six months or so. She had always dropped everything to come help us in the past, which was a true gift from God. Just knowing she was around to help with the house and the kids allowed me to stay focused on myself.

Claude also told me that he had decided to "embrace the disease." At that point, we both decided we needed to embrace the disease and educate more people about it. We had hope that my bipolar would continue to be managed.

Unfortunately, soon after the triathlon and our conversation, I would experience the worst episode I had ever had. Little did we know as we talked with each other that evening, in celebration of a momentous day, the pain and turmoil we were both about to endure.

Rejection Resurfaces

"I don't know what to do anymore. Can you please come over and talk to her?" Claude frantically begged Ingrid over the phone. After five years since I had first slipped Ingrid the note telling her how I felt inside, she had become a life line that we could call at any time. I'd often call her when negative thoughts were uncontrollable, and she'd encourage me the best she could. She and my friend Kimm continually supported me and helped me in my journey. At times, however, when I was really suicidal, I would isolate myself and not speak to anyone. After dealing with this mental anguish for nearly five years, this day was one of those times.

I was in complete despair. Ingrid came into my bedroom and found me curled up in a ball on the floor, cutting my wrist. Claude didn't know I had a weapon with which I could harm myself, but I had managed to dismantle a razor from our medicine cabinet with my bare hands. At that moment, I didn't care if I lived or died. I was tired of the roller coaster ride of emotions. Whenever it seemed like I had peace in my life, something would happen that would trigger me and send me in a downward spiral. I didn't always know exactly what the trigger was, but this time I did.

Due to all my Bible knowledge throughout the years, I was a good participant during our Bible studies, and I thirsted for more revelation from the Word of God. One day, I was at Fred and Ingrid's house for dinner, and I asked Fred if I could borrow some of his books to study the Word. Ingrid asked, "Why don't you take all that knowledge and teach Coffee Break sometime?" Coffee Break was the name of the Thursday morning study I attended at our church. I was thrilled that she asked me, as it was a dream of mine to be in that kind of teaching role.

While I was in France, I had taught French children some English and even traveled to Holland for a weekend to teach English there. I loved using my creative mind for good and always went above and beyond, trying to do things in excellence. It was the perfectionist in me, but being able to use my mind for something good was a bonus for me.

After Ingrid gave me that idea, I couldn't stop thinking about it. Not long after that evening, a woman I knew was going to teach a Bible study in the fall, and she asked me to be her co-leader. Finally, I could feel like a normal member of the church and not an outcast, even though I was never treated like an outcast. But then, something happened that caught me completely off-guard.

I was called into a meeting with all of the leaders. They explained to me in the most loving way that they felt it was not the right timing for me to be a co-leader. They believed I was still trying to gain stability, and they needed someone they could depend on to be there for all the women. I began sobbing during the meeting and told them it wasn't fair and they were persecuting me for being bipolar. "I didn't ask for this disease. It's not my fault that I have it!" I added for emphasis.

I understand now why the decision was made, but at the time, I still viewed life through the lens of rejection, and this was yet another reminder that I was defective. I lost all hope in that moment. I felt rejected, misunderstood, and disappointed in myself. *Maybe if I had a longer period of stability, they would've taken the risk to let me be a co-leader*, I thought. It was my fault. I blew it again!

We all hugged as we left, and I know they felt horrible. They didn't want to have to make that decision, and they didn't want to tell me. They all wished that I was well. They all wanted to see me healed and succeeding in life. We all wanted that, including myself, but no one knew how to get me there.

After Ingrid came into my bedroom, she sat on the floor next to me. She tried to talk to me and encourage me to stop cutting myself. She wanted to access where I was in my mind, although both she and Claude knew I was in a very dark place. After the recent rejection experience, the little hope I had held on to gradually diminished. My family deserved better than what I was capable of giving them. I was mad at God. Why did He give me this disease? I was trying to be used for His kingdom, and He rejected me. I knew deep down I was being punished because I couldn't stay sober and get my life together.

Rejection had always been my core issue. Being abandoned by both my mom and dad and others throughout my life took its toll on me. I was deeply affected as a little girl by the horrible choices my parents made. They were wounded themselves, and as a result, they ended up wounding us kids. Any real or imagined rejection set me off and propelled me rapidly downhill.

The women at church hadn't rejected me as a person, but that's not how I interpreted it. My mind said, "I am rejected." Additionally, the counselor I was seeing promised me that I could co-lead her groups in order to help others with bipolar disorder. I believed I'd be a good fit for it, but she never followed through, which devastated me yet again. I felt lied to and betrayed and rejected. I couldn't let it go, and I didn't know how to cope with the emotional pain. So, I did the only thing I knew how to do. I started slitting my wrist.

I heard Claude and Ingrid talking about taking me to the psych ward. I told them I didn't want to go because I was getting an A in my college course. For some reason, that class was my main concern. What would I tell my professor? What would he think? And, I didn't want to leave my kids again. But, deep down, I knew I was barely functioning. My mind was racing with thoughts of suicide, and I couldn't concentrate on anything else.

A Dark Night

Claude and Ingrid had decided to take me to the hospital, which ignited my anger. They made me pack a bag, for which I knew the drill. As I stormed downstairs, I began throwing my medication into my bag. I was so mad at both of them and for having to go to the hospital that I took a large handful of pills to retaliate. I didn't know how many I took, but I figured it wasn't enough to kill myself, only enough to cause concern, which it did.

Ingrid put me in her car, and we raced to the ER. I was silent as she attempted to talk some sense into me. At the ER, I had to tell the doctors about overdosing and show them my wrist. They weren't sure whether they needed to pump my stomach, and I tried to assure them they didn't. They decided to have me drink a glass of liquid charcoal to quickly absorb the pills I took. It was so disgusting tasting and absolutely torturous to drink. Then, for three days after I drank it, it continued to come out of my body!

As I lay on the hospital bed in the ER, Ingrid was at my side. I was concerned for Claude and the kids and felt so much guilt. I called Claude, but he was very distant in our conversation. Something had changed in him. He had been told that he was codependent and needed to show me tough love. As someone whose root issue is a fear of abandonment, being treated in a distant manner is traumatizing because it translates into being abandoned. I was terrified after talking to him, wondering if he would leave me.

I didn't blame him though. I would've certainly left me a long time ago. I was devastated thinking that maybe he would leave, and I might not get to see my kids. My children were my whole life. I longed for the days before my diagnoses, but I knew I couldn't go back. Here I was, in the ER, drinking charcoal because of an attempted suicide, with a bandage on my wrist, waiting to hear my fate yet again. I knew what it would be. I knew I'd soon be back in the psych ward.

In order to go to the psych ward, I had to take an ambulance across the street, and Ingrid wasn't allowed to take me. I entered the ambulance and lay down on the stretcher, saying goodbye to my friend. Soon I'd be all alone. Shame engulfed me once again. Why did I keep doing the same things over and over and over again? Why was I so crazy? Would I end up committing suicide? I knew the odds were good that I would.

As the ambulance pulled up to the hospital entrance after only five minutes, I had no idea what to expect, as I had not yet been to this particular psych ward. I did know that the plan was for me to go to this hospital's inpatient self-injury program as soon as I had stabilized. It would require me to be away from home for thirty days. The thought of that was traumatizing. I couldn't bear to think of the pain I was causing my children as they awoke the next morning.

I had always thought I would give my kids a far better life than I had. Moments like these were exactly what I was trying to prevent. I didn't want the cycle of dysfunction to repeat itself in my family, yet here it was. As I exited the ambulance, I was taken to a private room for evaluation. They noted all of my scars again to make sure I wasn't harming myself. It was hard knowing that I couldn't be trusted to be alone with myself. It was hard knowing that people feared leaving me alone. I was brought to my room, and for the time being, I was alone. I cried myself to sleep that night, which was not unusual. I also tried to read my Bible and pray. I cried out to God because I didn't know what else to do.

All Alone

The following day, the pain was unbearable. I went into the main room, picked up a schedule of things I was required to do, and stood in line to take my medication. All of our medication was kept behind the counter, and we were never allowed to administer it to ourselves. I was at the mercy of everyone in there. I had no freedoms anymore. I was trapped.

I had to meet with a new psychiatrist who would be in charge of managing my bipolar disorder medications while I was there. Again, I had to attend group therapy, eat meals in a cafeteria sitting alone because I didn't know anyone, and meet with a psychiatrist and counselor. On that first day, I tried calling my friends for support. Just like Claude, they were distant. They had all banded together to show me tough love. It was crushing to me. I began experiencing the pains of rejection and abandonment all over again.

I believed that everyone would leave me this time around, even though they said they wouldn't. That fear caused even more depression, anxiety, and suicidal thinking while I was in the hospital. I couldn't talk about this in my group therapy, though, or they'd keep me longer. I had to hold it in.

Instead, I called Elizabeth. I was so thankful to have someone to talk to. Elizabeth had a motherly way about her, and I had craved a nurturing, mother figure in my life for years. Speaking to Elizabeth was uplifting, but as soon as I hung up the phone, loneliness overwhelmed me.

Getting into the self-injury program at the hospital wasn't easy. I was put on a waiting list, and my insurance needed to be approved. Realizing that my entry into the program was out of my hands, I knew I had to do whatever I could to help myself get well. I discovered a voluntary chapel service that was offered, and I wanted to be involved with anything that had to do with God.

Several of us walked into the service where the chaplain was waiting for us. She gave us a warm smile as we took our seats. As I sat, I noticed a sheet of paper with music lyrics on my seat. The chaplain opened in prayer, and I started getting tears in my eyes. I never felt so lonely in my life, along with every other negative emotion I've ever experienced. It all hit me at once.

We began singing, "Great Is Thy Faithfulness," and I sobbed uncontrollably. I wanted to go home. I wanted to be well. I wanted this to end. I truly wanted to believe in the faithfulness of God to give me the peace I desired, but I didn't have any faith that I'd ever get there based on the doctors' reports and the research that I did on bipolar disorder. And, I had no faith because it seemed like nothing I did was working. I did everything everyone asked me to do. I was doing all the "right" things to get better, yet I wasn't. I continued to sing about how faithful God was, all the while feeling depressed and hopeless and longing like never before to go home and be with my family.

I wanted to prove to my friends and family once and for all that I would never relapse or self-injure again. I wanted to show them that I could be a great wife, mother, and friend, and make up for the painful times that I had caused everyone.

We took Communion during the service, and I knew I needed a lot of time to repent for all the sins I'd committed. I knew I was a dirty, rotten sinner who couldn't stop sinning. I felt like I was disappointing God every time I failed. It was impossible for me to remember every sin, so I simply said, "Please forgive me for all the sins I don't remember doing." I took Communion, yet still felt imprisoned by the guilt and shame that held me captive.

CHAPTER 14

LIFE IN A SELF-INJURY PROGRAM

While waiting to get accepted into the self-injury program, I met a girl in the psych ward with whom I'd watch movies and talk. It helped me pass the time, even though many of the movies triggered sadness for me, reminding me that life wasn't all roses. The movies tended to have uplifting endings with people loving and supporting each other. The characters were normal people with normal lives, and they reminded me how abnormal my life and I were.

My new friend and I often ate meals together in the cafeteria, which kept me from looking like a complete outcast. Some of those in the program did eat by themselves, always looking down, never making eye contact. It was sad to watch them talk to themselves. In the psych ward, everyone was constantly watched. There was no escaping the "ever-seeing eyes." The only way I could be alone was in my room, which wasn't allowed at certain times. We were forced to follow their programs, and they didn't want us in isolation all day. It was tiring.

But, finally, the day came when I learned I was going to be transferred to the self-injury program in the same hospital. I was excited to graduate out of the psych ward into something I felt was a little more "acceptable." I knew I needed help with my self-injury addiction, and this program was so well respected that people came from all parts of the country to be in it, hence my need to be on the waitlist. It was regarded as a place of healing for self-destructive addiction, as well as eating disorders. Most of those who self-injure also have an eating disorder.

Once I was in the program, I had my own room until I was placed with a roommate. I cherished the alone time where I could cry myself to sleep. I knew that I'd be shedding many more tears until I eventually went home. At my first group session, there were about twenty of us in the room. Looking around, I noticed that most of the girls were teenagers. In some ways, it was not surprising, as most people who self-injure are young and eventually grow out of it. There were two other older women, so at least I wasn't the only adult.

As we took turns speaking that day, we were asked to share our feelings, which caused me to begin sobbing, as I explained how I missed my kids and I wanted to go home. When I was in the psych ward, Claude thought it'd be best to not visit me with the kids, and it hurt my heart. I didn't want my children to think that I had abandoned them, at least intentionally.

I had been told that this program was intense and included twelve hours of daily group therapy, psychiatric appointments, homework, and other activities. We even had to write papers. I was hopeful that just maybe this program would help me. I knew that here, I could freely talk about self-injury without people feeling turned off and disgusted. They understood and wouldn't judge me. I made a decision to do the best I could in the program and do everything they asked of me.

Learning to Adjust

"It's time for your vitals!" a woman loudly proclaimed in the middle of the night, charging through my door to take my blood pressure and temperature. Her intrusion was a nightly occurrence for two weeks, while I was considered an inpatient. This was a thirty-day program, including two weeks of inpatient and two weeks of outpatient therapy, where I'd leave the hospital at night and come back the next morning. My goal was to stay at home after two weeks then drive to the program in the mornings, since I only lived twenty minutes away. Being startled awake in the middle of each night was not something I was looking forward to!

The first morning, I headed off to a group session. I felt like the odd one there because most of the girls already had a chance to get to know each other and were talking together. They had allowed one of the girls to run the first session, and she began by telling us to share how we were feeling. Our words were then written on a dry erase board for everyone to see. We also had to set a goal for the day. They passed around a sheet of paper that had a list of various feelings.

At the time, it was foreign to me to have to examine and discuss how I felt. I could typically choose maybe three feelings, but this sheet listed over a hundred different ways we could express ourselves. It was hard for me to choose. I had to dig deep into my emotions—not an easy task. We did this exercise every day for thirty days, so I eventually learned to express myself in various ways, which was healthy.

We also attended many therapy sessions daily. In these groups, horrendous stories of abuse, hurt, betrayal, loss of loved ones, addictions, mental illness, and trauma came forth. Tears were shed, anger was released, and compassion was displayed toward one another. We knew we were all there for a reason, and we tried to come alongside each other. Over time, we older members became mother figures for the younger.

During my free time, I'd do homework, then go to my room to be alone so I could read the Bible as much as possible. As I read, God touched my heart. The girls tried to get me to stay with them and participate in activities, but I just wanted to be alone with the Lord. I knew I needed Him every minute of every day, and if I didn't depend on Him, I'd never make it. As a result of wanting to be alone, I was persecuted. The girls accused me of being "too good" for them and stuck up. This certainly wasn't true, and I tried to explain to them my reasoning behind my alone time, but they didn't want to listen.

The most difficult part of being in the program was the visiting hours, which came several times a week at night. Usually, I was one of the only few who didn't have visitors. It was extremely painful. I felt like an outcast, which only solidified my beliefs of being abnormal, defective, and unlovable. I know Claude was doing the best he could and that my friends thought this would make me think twice about relapsing again, so they believed that distancing themselves from me was a good thing. They thought tough love was the best approach. But it wasn't a good thing; I felt abandoned in my time of need. I just wanted to feel loved.

The time that I needed my support system the most is the time that I felt the most lonely. I was trying hard to heal and recover, but the abandonment only resurfaced the suicidal thoughts. I knew I wouldn't survive feeling so rejected and alone. At some point I believed I'd most likely take my own life. I couldn't continue to keep causing pain and chaos for my family and friends.

During visiting hours, I ended up bonding with a young girl. She was from out of state and didn't have anyone to visit her. We'd sit in the hallway and talk. I became a mother figure to her and spoke life into her as much as possible. She was only thirteen, and it broke my heart to see her in so much pain at such a young age. I talked with her about the Lord, and He would use me to encourage her. He used me in the darkest places to speak to others. I didn't realize it at the time, but I was His instrument to reach into others' hurting lives.

Whenever I could, I'd take advantage of my alone time to be with God. I'd hug my Bible like a stuffed animal and cry myself to sleep with it. I'd plead to the Father for help and hold my Bible for dear life. I believe that during these times, the Holy Spirit was speaking to me and showing me that my only hope was to discover the truth in His Word that would someday change my world. God was my only hope, and holding my Bible and squeezing it helped me feel His presence. It helped me believe I wasn't alone, but that God was my friend in my time of need.

Kicked Out

"I can't let you come back home this time," Claude said sternly. I held the phone in shock and disbelief and asked, "What did you just say?" He repeated himself word for word, then added, "Not only can't you come home at night, but you'll need to find a place to live for several months." I was completely devastated and heartbroken. I tried everything I could think of to change Claude's mind, but nothing worked.

He then talked to me about a halfway house, where recovering addicts and alcoholics live with others in order to help them gradually assimilate back into society. I didn't want to think about that. I just wanted to go back home and be with my kids. I would've been away almost nine weeks after the program and was looking forward to going back to a "normal" life.

I knew he wouldn't change his mind, and I figured someone must've been coaching him in this. Of course, I immediately began thinking that everyone was talking about me and mad at me and that they still thought I was crazy. I knew I'd continue to be the outcast at church. His response angered me, and in times of anger, I'd isolate myself by putting up a wall, which only proved to be self-defeating. It simply made my negative emotions worse, as I stewed in the mire of unforgiveness, bitterness, and retaliation.

I didn't trust that people — even my own husband at times — had my best interests at heart. I had to somehow learn to change my mind from "Everyone's out to get me," to "We all fail, including me. My friends and family do have my best interests at heart. They're not out to get me." All of the programs and therapy sessions I attended were based on helping us relearn thought patterns about ourselves and others. I was slowly relearning to rewire my brain from negative thoughts to positive. But, it was a process and not something that would happen quickly.

After my conversation with Claude, I started asking around to get information about where I could live. The realization hit me that I was actually homeless; I had nowhere to go. My shame and guilt increased. The fear of rejection and abandonment worsened, as I had been kicked out of my own home. I knew deep down that Claude was only trying his best to protect himself and the kids, but I viewed it as rejection because I was born bipolar. I didn't ask to have this disease. It wasn't fair. If I had cancer instead, I'd be welcomed home. People would visit me in the hospital, and I would be treated equally to others.

The truth is, Jesus loves all those with mental illness. He has nothing but compassion on the torment they're experiencing, and He wants to love them into a place of freedom. They're sick and need Dr. Jesus as much as someone who has a physical illness. They don't need to be treated as "less than" or be tossed aside. They need stable love from God and others who will love them like Christ! If Jesus were on the earth, He'd be hanging out in psych wards, loving on all the patients.

After much searching, I found a place known as a three-quarter house instead of a halfway house that could take me after my program. I was both relieved and scared. I didn't want to go, but I had no other place to live. I decided that I needed to do whatever my husband thought was best so that I could ultimately be with him and my children.

Passing the Time

Throughout the self-injury program, I had a lot of therapy, psychiatric appointments, medication changes, and homework. In many ways, being there was like living in a four-week soap opera. Some of the girls in the program didn't want to be there and get help. They were only there because they were forced to be. Because of that, many would hide their medication and not take it. Then, after a time of accumulating it, they'd crush it up and snort it to get high. One girl snuck her ear piercing tool in and secretly pierced the ears of willing victims during visiting hours' sessions. And, then, of course, there was the drama of girls regularly fighting with each other and forming childish cliques. It reminded me of a college environment in many ways, and I wanted to escape to be with adults again.

One of the girls there was quite mean and known for bullying. I know she was wounded, and her pain manifested as wanting to control everyone else. One day during our gym time, we were all playing volleyball. I was going easy on the group, even though I knew I could play well and hit hard. The bully wasn't taking it easy though. She was on the opposite team, and at one point we were across the net from one another.

After my teammate served the ball, it returned from the other side, and when it came to me, I spiked it as hard as I could. It hit the bully right in the face, knocking her to the ground. I didn't intend to hurt anyone, and I immediately became concerned. They called for a nurse, who determined the bully would be alright, but she was wheeled back to our floor in a wheelchair.

I wondered if this girl was going to retaliate somehow, and I became somewhat fearful. But, instead of retaliating, she started respecting me.

I believe that, in the moment of spiking the ball, I was symbolically standing up for all those who felt they were being abused and bullied. I guess I had stored up my anger, and it came down on the volleyball that day! I'm glad the bully ended up being okay, but I'm also glad that I stood up to her for the rest of us, even though hurting her was unintentional.

I also tried to pass the time by crocheting. I had learned to knit and crochet as a child, but I had forgotten how. Someone in my program knew how and re-taught me. I decided to make a baby doll blanket for my girls as a way to show them my love while I was away. I poured all my effort and love into making the best doll blankets possible. I couldn't wait to give them to my girls when they came to visit.

Claude and the kids did come see me a couple of times. Once, Claude's mother came with them. She pulled me aside, looked me straight in the eyes, and said, "You need to stop self-injuring for the sake of the kids." I replied simply, "Yes, I know." The shame was overwhelming. My mother-in-law, who was very cultured and from a nice family, was here to help us because her daughter-in-law was severely mentally ill. I knew she had to have told her family all about it. There must've been shame on their end as well to have to break it to the rest of the family.

Claude's family was the exact opposite of mine. I felt I had failed to live up to their expectations. My mother-in-law had so much pain in her eyes as she said that to me. I could sense her compassion on our family, and I was deeply touched, yet felt so guilty for being the cause of my family's pain.

Worst. Mother. Ever.

"It's an emergency; it's your husband," the program director stated matter-of-factly, handing me the phone. My heart raced as I took it from her, while my mind swirled with thoughts over what the emergency might be. Tiphanie, our oldest daughter, was in the hospital with a nasal infection, Claude explained. She needed antibiotics and would have to stay in the hospital for a couple of days. Fortunately, the hospital was right next to my building.

At this point in the program, I could go to a hotel for two weeks in the evenings. I had to be on site from 8 A.M. to 8 P.M. each day, and then I'd take a van with some others to a hotel where we were allowed to stay overnight. We were shuttled back to the program in the morning. Because I was free to leave in the evenings, I told Claude that I'd walk to the hospital to see Tiphanie and my family.

Claude became enraged with me on the phone. "You should be here, and you're not!" he yelled. "It's hard for me to work full time and take care of the kids. You should be here." I didn't know how to respond to him. He was right. I should've been there. I was the mother. I had been a stay-at-home mom for years, and Claude relied on me until my life fell apart. I hung up the phone, trembling with anxiety. I was worried about my daughter, and I was worried that Claude would leave me and I'd lose my children. This was a very real possibility. Suicidal thinking arose with a vengeance in that moment, but I couldn't tell anyone.

I went back to the evening's program sessions, but Tiphanie was heavy on my mind. As soon as my commitments ended, I ran to the hospital. When I arrived on her floor, there was an intercom, and I needed to be "buzzed" in. I announced into the speaker, "It's Nichole Marbach. I'm here to see Tiphanie Marbach." The woman on the other end asked, "Who are you?" It saddened me that she didn't realize I was Tiphanie's mother. I felt like an intruder.

When I walked into my daughter's room, I saw the stares from the nurses, which said to me, "You should have been there." I knew Claude had told them about me and my situation, and it was difficult to see the way they looked at me and how they acted when I came in the room. I walked over and hugged Tiphanie. It was tough to be in the same room with Claude, the kids, and my mother-in-law. I could feel the resentment toward me for not being there. I felt like I had a sticker stamped to my head that read, "Worst mother in the world!"

I learned that my neighbors had come to visit Tiphanie and had brought her gifts. They must've known that I was away from home, and the news spread throughout my neighborhood. I knew that I would now be considered the mentally ill, crazy one, who no one could trust with their kids. In that moment, I didn't know how to act. I could tell that Claude's anger and resentment was boiling. He, too, had enough of this life of torment. And I didn't blame him one bit.

The time came for Claude to drive me to the hotel so I could be at my program the next day, and my mother-in-law had to leave with our two other children. One of my daughters cried because she wanted to stay with Claude. There was nothing but pain for my entire family during this time, and there was no denying it. In some ways, we had all lost hope in a better future. My condition was really taking a toll on our family.

I tried to be strong as I said goodbye to Tiphanie, then Claude and I walked to the car and drove to the hotel. For the first time ever in our marriage, he said to me, "I don't know why I'm still married to you," and he began talking about the possibility of divorce. My heart sank. Could my greatest fears be coming true? I had no idea how to respond, so I just let him vent. It was difficult to face reality in that moment. I know I couldn't guarantee my husband a life without bipolar cycles. And I couldn't guarantee that I'd never feel suicidal again or attempt to take my life. I couldn't guarantee anything at that point.

When we arrived at the hotel, I proceeded directly to my room where I cried my eyes out. I talked with the Lord, who was my best friend. I also called my AA sponsor, and she helped encourage me. I had to meet with my program therapist the following day, but I didn't share that I was feeling suicidal. What I needed was to get out of the program and go home, but I couldn't tell her that. I only told her positive things that would help my case and give me a good report.

The next morning, some of the girls in the program were watching cartoons, and it broke my heart. They were the same cartoons I'd watch with my kids, and I was again reminded how I was away from home when I should've been there. Every time I saw the cartoons on, I had to leave the room. These girls weren't mothers and didn't have the responsibility of thinking of anyone other than themselves. Because of that, many didn't take the program seriously.

But, I had a family, which made it much harder to be there. I wanted help. I wanted to be well. I took it seriously. My heart broke for those girls, not knowing how they would end up. But it also broke for me and the damage I had caused my own girls. Would things ever be normal for my family again?

CHAPTER 15

THE BEGINNING OF THE END

My first thought upon looking around my new home away from home—the recovery home—was how many books it had. In the first room I entered, there were several shelves lined with books. I figured that the women who had stayed in the house left their books for those who came after them. I loved seeing all the books, as I wanted to try to pass as much time as possible as fast as possible so I could finally go home.

When I first arrived in the house, I was told that my room was upstairs. I also soon learned that my roommate was someone no one liked. She was an older lady, who apparently wasn't very happy. Once in my room, I slowly unpacked the few articles of clothing and other material items I had and tried to make my area as comfortable as possible. I knew I would need to be strong and stick it out here for several months, so I wanted to try to enjoy the space I was given.

I met the other ladies in the home, and they were friendly, but since I was the newcomer, I knew I'd have to earn their trust. I discovered that we had chores we were required to do, as well as go to AA meetings and meet with the in-home therapist. I also learned that I needed to find a job or do volunteer work in order to stay in the home. I thought that might be difficult because I didn't have a car. Claude didn't want me to have a car while I was there, and I was the only one without "wheels." I had to rely on the other women to take me wherever I needed to go. If I couldn't get a ride, then I walked. I had never been without a car in my life since the day I could drive.

It was also hard for me to live with women I didn't know. We had a sign-in/sign-out sheet at the front door to know where everyone was at all times. And, because I was new, I wasn't allowed to leave for long periods of time, unless it was for a job or volunteering.

One of the first things I did was to try to get a job. I walked to the local restaurant and talked to the manager about work, since I had years of waitressing experience as a teenager. I thought for sure I'd be hired, but I wasn't. I then filled out applications at the local supermarket, coffee shop, and wherever else I could, but no one hired me. I had finally completed my bachelor's degree in French and international business a couple of years back, but even with that and work experience, I still couldn't get hired at a minimum wage job. Not having a car was a liability because I was limited in the places I could work.

I had met a woman from the home, however, who worked at a thrift store, and I was able to volunteer there with her. I wasn't paid, but at least I could do something. My job was to sort through the clothing donations, tag them, then hang them up. It was definitely humbling to go from a stay-at-home mom to volunteering in a thrift shop away from my family.

I gave the job my all, and the woman I worked for was impressed with my effort. I felt like I was at least contributing somewhere to help people. I tried to do everything with excellence, no matter what it was I was doing. Volunteering at the thrift shop allowed me to continue to live in the recovery home, which was a blessing, as it would eventually help me get back home—if I stayed there for the time that was required of me.

"Mommy, Are You Still Sick?"

My most painful memory at the recovery home was when Claude came to pick me up with our children so we could be together as a family. We went to the park and attempted to bring a sense of normalness back to our family. We had a great visit, but then came the dreaded moment of having to go back to the house and leave everyone. It broke my heart, especially because I didn't get many visits from them. It was too painful and confusing for the kids and too difficult for us all to say goodbye.

My son, our youngest, had always been a mama's boy. He melted my heart, and we bonded from the start. He didn't understand what was going on with me or why I wasn't living at home. On that day, as I was getting out of the car, he looked up at me from his car seat, and asked, "Mommy, are you still sick?" My heart sank like an anchor. I felt so much pain and grief that I wanted to run from the car and sob. I just wanted to hug him tightly and take him places and pretend like none of this ever happened, but I couldn't.

I carried so much continual guilt for being a mentally ill mother with addictions. I didn't know how to be well; I didn't know how to be sane again. *How could I simply fall apart one day and become such a completely different person?* was a question that often ran through my mind. I was unable to extend myself love and grace and see that the years of abuse and trauma were what had caused me to be sick. It didn't happen overnight. Years of wrong thinking and viewing my life through the lens of rejection had caused this living hell.

I was strong for my son when he asked me that question, and I promised him that I would be well soon and back at home. I said my goodbyes and returned to the house crying. The suicidal thinking arose again, as I considered how my kids would be better off without a mother who wasn't stable enough to give them the love and attention they deserved. I desired to be the best mom in the world, and I tried for many years, but the reality was that I was incapable of being the mother I wanted to be. It hurt my heart deeply, and I suffered with the realization alone.

Home Sweet Home

Over time, Claude saw that I was doing everything necessary to get better. Because of that, he allowed me to have a car. It was wonderful to be driving again, and I felt like a sixteen-year-old who just got her license! I learned not to take driving for granted anymore. Having the freedom to drive was a privilege, and I wanted to savor the moment.

Aside from helping at the thrift store, I was able to drive to volunteer at my church. I also picked up some odd jobs, such as landscaping work and a painting job from one of my friends. I was actually able to pay the rent for the house with my own income. Knowing that my medical visits were costing us a fair amount of money, I wanted to help pay back the bills I had incurred.

Claude and I had talked about me spending some time at home while I was still at the recovery house. I had earned more time away and was able to spend the night at my own house from time to time. The first day I drove home was a beautiful sunny day, and my neighbor was sitting outside enjoying the weather. As I walked over to talk with her, I noticed other neighbors go past me and stare. I knew they'd all soon be talking about me: "Did you see Nichole?" "Is she back home now?" I knew there'd be fresh gossip at my expense, but I honestly didn't care anymore. It was too important for me to be home with my family. Like driving, I didn't want to take my family for granted. I wanted to cherish every second spent with them.

My new focus was on my family. I knew I'd have the support of my church family, so I didn't feel the need to be best friends with the neighbors. Instead, I needed to stay in environments that were safe for me. Church was safe; the neighborhood wasn't, except for my one neighbor. She had come to visit me at the self-injury program once and brought me a coffee. It was nice to see her, and her gesture showed that she loved and cared for me and wouldn't shun me like others had. Whenever we needed anything, we could call each other and be there for one another. She was the one neighbor I knew I could always count on—a true gift from God.

Being home after being gone for so long was also a gift from God. I was thrilled just to feel a little bit normal again. Then the time came for me to leave the recovery house, and I couldn't have been more overjoyed! I left and never looked back. I made it! I told myself I'd never allow myself to ever go that low again. My hope had returned.

A Very Different Kind of Meeting

As I moved back home and we all adjusted to me being back, I continued with therapy, psychiatric appointments, church, Bible studies, and AA meetings. I started accepting more and more that this would be my new way of life, and I could never go back to the old. I had no choice but to accept it.

At one AA meeting I attended, I learned about a new meeting held in the same building. It was called a Dual Diagnosis Recovery meeting. I wanted to try it, thinking that maybe it was something I had been missing in my recovery. The meeting was specifically for those with mental illness and addictions. I convinced myself I should attend when I noticed another bipolar cycle revving up, and I started getting scared.

At the first meeting, I met Tanya, also bipolar and alcoholic — but, more importantly, a Christian. Tanya and I exchanged phone numbers, and I eventually asked her to become my new sponsor. I knew that I needed a sponsor who understood the entire bipolar piece. She accepted, leading us to have coffee together from time to time. I realized that I bonded with her in a way that I hadn't with others because I knew she was a Christian.

Tanya invited me to go to a Christian-based recovery meeting with her, but I declined. I figured I had enough meetings on my plate and didn't want to add another. But, she didn't give up asking, and the next time, I felt that God wanted me to say yes. She told me there was a female leader in the program named Anita who was a psychiatric nurse. She wanted us to meet because she could see that Anita had a lot of compassion on the mentally ill. Tanya had raved about her and couldn't wait to introduce us. We decided to go together to visit her the following week.

I noticed a difference immediately upon entering Anita's meeting. She was genuinely welcoming toward me, and those in the group were friendly and accepting. We began the meeting with a time of worship, and I was thankful that they made God the focus. After worship, we broke into groups based on our various issues. I kept quiet in my group until we had to introduce ourselves. I stated that I was a bipolar alcoholic and that it was my first time attending. I sat quietly and listened to everyone with my head down.

Even though I didn't participate, I enjoyed my time there and told Tanya as much. The following day, I began corresponding with Anita. I let her know that the meeting was powerful and that it blessed me, while also filling her in on all of my diagnoses. She continued to respond to me and encourage me as I wrote to her during the week, always pointing me to the Lord. The next week I returned to her group, feeling safe with both her and Tanya.

After a couple of weeks, Anita told me that I'd have to count off like everyone else, and if there were too many people, I might have to leave her group and go to another leader, Lisa's, group. Each week, everyone counted off in twos then split into two groups. That night, I ended up in Lisa's group.

When the group began, I instantly saw something in Lisa that I wanted. I knew that she had a real, intimate relationship with the Lord, and I yearned for that. I desired to know God the way she knew Him. I realized that there was so much more to Him than I had ever known. As she talked, I started to feel comfortable, like I was in a safe place. As the group continued, I decided to admit to everyone about my past, including the brief relapse I had in the short period of time that I had been back home.

The encouragement I received from Lisa was life-giving encouragement to show me that God was not disappointed in me. It was encouragement to tell me that I could do all things through Christ who strengthens me. It focused on who I was in Christ. Instead of hanging my head in my usual shame, I lifted my head as she spoke and looked her straight in the eyes. She continued speaking life into my wounded heart. I left that night sensing a new wind at my back and much needed hope for my future.

Words of Life

Even though I still kept razor blades and pills in my purse (just in case), I continued attending the Christian recovery group and stayed in regular contact with Anita and Lisa. I also still battled racing, anxiety-filled thoughts and struggled with depression. But, I had moments of peace as well, when I was at their meetings or receiving the truth from them. They were passionate about the Lord in a way I'd never seen, and I wanted that same passion. I desperately wanted what they had, so I listened to all they kept sharing with me.

One day, after a meeting had ended and we were all downstairs enjoying some refreshments, I had a moment alone with Lisa. I'll never forget her looking at me with great compassion and love. Beginning to tear up, she said, "I know God has a mighty destiny for you. I just know it." I was so touched by her words that came straight from the Father's heart and spoke life and encouragement to me. Her words struck me to the core.

At that moment, I truly believed that God really did love me enough to have her say that to me. I knew that Lisa was hearing from God. Right then, the Holy Spirit spoke to my spirit as well, saying, "Nichole, it's true." Lisa had looked at me and saw who I was in Christ. For once, someone didn't just see me as a bipolar, alcoholic failure. She didn't let the mess in my life deter her from speaking God's destiny to me. For once, someone saw me as Christ saw me and realized the potential that God had deposited into me since before I was even born.

People need to hear life-giving, hope-filled words for their future, even when their lives and circumstances appear to be a giant mess. People need to keep hope alive in their heart. I thank God for the people He sent into my life at just the right time, as they forever changed my life. Their life-giving words straight from God's heart became the catalyst that set me on my new path of freedom.

PART III

TRIUMPH

CHAPTER 16

THE TRUTH WILL SET YOU FREE

Sitting in my car in a Walmart parking lot, I checked email on my phone. I had been corresponding with Anita via email, sharing with her my various diagnoses. I knew I could trust her because she was a psychiatric nurse. I told her about the battle that constantly raged in my emotions, so she knew I was fighting depression, along with other negativity.

I had assumed she would tell me what all the others had, which was that my diagnoses are all incurable. Instead, I sat stunned as I read her words: "With God all things are possible. Everything is possible with Him." Her words resonated with my spirit. I thought, *Yes, that's true. I know that scripture is in the Bible. I know that's truth.*

I felt excitement and hope begin to well up inside of me. This is the answer I had been waiting for! I read her words again and pondered them for a couple of minutes. Then I began to cry. *God is the God of the impossible. He can heal me and do the impossible,* I said to myself. As I read further, Anita said something to me that completely transformed my life and began a journey of healing within me that I'm still on today.

She told me, "The enemy comes to steal, kill, and destroy, and he's trying to steal and kill and destroy your life." She was referring to John 10:10—"The thief comes only to steal and kill and destroy; I have come that they may have life, and have it to the full" (NIV). I didn't know a lot about the devil, but I realized in that moment that he was the one responsible for wreaking havoc in my life through abandonment, rejection, and abuse. For years, I had listened to his lies that I was a horrible person who didn't deserve the love of friends and family. These lies of unworthiness and self-hatred had prevented me from receiving the love of God and the love of those around me. The enemy had succeeded in making me feel insignificant and "less than" my whole life. And, in my ignorance, I fell for it.

But no longer. I finally understood why I had been doing all that I was told to do but not seeing any results. This was the missing piece to my puzzle. I believe that all the prayers over the years on my behalf were being answered in that very moment. I knew that my friends, family, and church had prayed countless prayers for me to find peace and to be kept safe. At this point in time, the Holy Spirit imparted to me a righteous anger against the enemy with this life-changing revelation: "I am a child of God, and I don't have to take this anymore!"

Jesus came to give me a full, abundant life, and I wasn't living that life. If He wanted me to have a full life, He wouldn't have given me a mental disease that caused me suicidal thinking. That didn't make sense. I was God's beloved whom He was willing to die for. I was loved and cherished by Him. The enemy was the one harassing me and tormenting me. I realized now, without a shadow of a doubt, that most of the voices I was hearing were not my own—especially those voices of self-hatred and condemnation. The enemy was the one telling me to kill myself. He was the one telling me to cut myself. He was the one who held me hostage with shame and guilt.

No more! He had been found out. I would have to take a stand against those negative voices whenever they tried to come back. I was angry that I had been duped all those years. And, I was angry that even though I read the Bible, I never saw this truth. At the same time, I was excited! I had always known that there was more truth in the Word than I knew, and this only proved it.

I wept that day with tears of joy and hope. I grabbed hold of hope that day—real hope—and have never let it go! I was experiencing joy, excitement, and sorrow all at once. The sorrow was regret for all the torment I had to go through before I received God's truth. But I knew it was now time to move forward and not dwell on the past. It was time for a new adventure!

My New and Final Label

I realized deep in my heart that day, that my identity was now "child of God." Healing belonged to me, and in God's power, I could continue to stand against the enemy who was trying to destroy my life through lies and deception. The labels of bipolar disorder, borderline personality disorder, PTSD, and ADD were gone for good. I was not an alcoholic, a binge eater, or a self-injurer. My new label was "child of God," and it was the only label I would ever need.

Although "child of God" had been my identity ever since I accepted Jesus as a little girl, I didn't know it. Because I didn't know it, I ignorantly accepted any label that doctors or counselors wanted to put on me. But now, in my spirit, I knew that I knew that I knew that God's Word was true and His identity for me was true. No one—not even the devil—could take that knowledge away from me or change my mind.

In that moment, John 8:32—"Then you will know the truth, and the truth will set you free" (NIV)—came to pass personally in my life. I believe that when the revelation of these words and the understanding of who I am in Christ came to me, the spiritual forces of darkness that had been harassing me left. No one was there to pray for me. It was the revelation of the truth of God's Word that set me free!

The truth was that Jesus had pronounced me worthy of love. He had declared that I was healed by His stripes that He endured on the cross. He said, "… as he is, so are we in this world" (1 John 4:17, KJV), and I knew that Jesus didn't experience mental torment. He had peace; therefore, I could have peace. Jesus knew who He was, and He knew He was radically loved and accepted by His Father. The Holy Spirit spoke to me that day, telling me the same thing. When we know how much the Father loves us and accepts us, we won't get tricked into believing the lies of the enemy or the lies we tell ourselves.

I was ready to receive this truth. All the love that I had received over the years from my friends and family had prepared me for this moment. I knew that if something didn't change in my life, I wouldn't be alive much longer. According to the Depression and Bipolar Support Alliance, bipolar disorder takes an average of

9.2 years off of a person's life (dbsalliance.org). I'm certain this is due to the anxiety and stress it inflicts. Not having peace takes a toll!

I finally had more hope than I had ever had in my life, and I knew I'd keep holding on to this hope no matter what. This was real hope—God's hope. Not the false hope that I had before. I truly knew that these diseases weren't mine anymore. They didn't belong to me as a child of God. I left the Walmart parking lot a changed person, as a deep transformation began taking place on the inside.

I also believe that, at that moment, my brain was supernaturally healed, and the chemicals in it became normal. A miracle took place that day, and no one could ever take that away from me. With the help of the Holy Spirit, I chose to believe the Word of God over the doctors' reports. I knew now, that despite what I had been told for years, bipolar disorder was curable. The cure is Jesus! He pronounced me healed and whole.

I am God's child in whom He is well pleased. I am a new creation in Jesus. I am worthy of God's love and the love of those around me. This is what mattered to me now. From this moment on, I needed to grow in these truths that would ultimately set my mind completely free and bring me into a brand-new life.

Walking in My Healing

While I believe that God miraculously healed me, I don't believe that He had been holding out on me and waiting for a certain day to bring His healing to pass in my life. His healing had been mine for the taking all along. I was the one who had hindered His healing because of my wrong beliefs! When I finally understood what He had done for me and received it as truth into my life, my healing journey began. That's what happened that day in the Walmart parking lot. But it was just the beginning.

I still had a long way to go in order to fully walk out my healing; in fact, I'm still in the process of doing so. I still fail sometimes by believing things that are no longer true of me. I still have to stand against lies from time to time over things like rejection and inferiority. But the difference now is that I know who I am in Christ, and I know that I don't have to listen to the lies anymore. While some aspects of my healing were instantaneous, other parts required me to completely change my beliefs toward God, His Word, and my identity in Him.

The best way I knew how to do this was to dive into as many books on God's healing and our power of authority in Christ as possible. Once I began this process, I didn't want to stop. There were so many scriptures that either I didn't know were in the Bible or I didn't know how to correctly interpret. One important truth I learned is that healing is ours through Jesus Christ and that God is no respecter of persons. He doesn't pick and choose whom He heals. Instead, healing is a finished work because of Jesus' crucifixion. Isaiah 53:5 reads, "But He was wounded for our transgressions, He was crushed for our wickedness [our sin, our injustice, our wrongdoing]; the punishment [required] for our well-being *fell* on Him, and by His stripes (wounds) we are healed" (AMP).

I realized this truth the day that God told me while I was self-injuring and watching my blood flow, "You don't have to do that anymore because My Son shed His blood for you." God was trying to tell me that I was already healed by the stripes and wounds of Jesus. His blood had healed me and set me free! I qualified for healing because of Jesus — not because of my behavior.

In the Bible, Mary Magdalene had seven demons cast out of her (Mark 16:9). After her miraculous healing, she was with Jesus constantly and followed Him wherever she could. She was finally free from the torment, so she now lived a life of gratitude to Jesus, her Savior. I completely understand how Mary must've felt. I had so much gratitude knowing that I didn't have to live with mental torment for the rest of my life. I felt like I could finally be the wife and mother I'd always dreamed of being. I talked to Jesus all the time now and shared His healing with everyone I could.

When I returned to church, people noticed I was different. I was glowing with God's peace and joy. I now walked with my head up instead of down. I walked with a new confidence that I never had before. People I didn't even know but just passed by at church would pull me aside and ask, "What happened to you?" They wanted to know how I got free. They wanted to know what made the difference. I couldn't stop sharing the truth of what I learned. Some people were quite interested, while others weren't sure of my revelation that healing was for everyone.

It wasn't my responsibility to change what they thought; I was simply supposed to share what happened to me. I told everyone that I had been healed! Even though I was still reluctantly taking medication, I knew beyond a doubt that I was healed. I also knew that one day soon, I would no longer be taking any medication.

Understanding that the enemy was trying to steal, kill, and destroy my life and that I didn't need to put up with it anymore was a life-changing revelation that set me free. But it wasn't enough to just know this. I had to put this revelation into practice. When anxiety tried to grip me, I had to fight it off. I now understood that my fight was spiritual, not physical, and I had to use the authority that Jesus has given His followers to keep anxiety from taking hold of me (Luke 10:19). To exercise His authority, I'd speak out loud, "In the name of Jesus, anxiety, leave me. You have no right in my life."

I knew I could do this because of Mark 11:23, where Jesus said, "Truly I tell you, if anyone says to this mountain, 'Go, throw yourself into the sea,' and does not doubt in their heart but believes that what they say will happen, it will be done for them" (NIV). Our mountains can be symptoms of sickness. We have authority over those symptoms in Christ, and that was one of the missing pieces I didn't understand until my healing. If we don't know that we have the delegated authority of Jesus over sickness, we won't exercise it. Through Jesus, we can take authority over any mountains in our life.

As I spoke to the anxiety with the authority that Jesus has given believers, it would leave. I did this with other things in my life too, like fear. Fear will always try to come upon us in different ways as long as we're on the earth, but I knew that even in the times when such things did try to come back on me, it didn't mean that I wasn't healed. I knew I was healed!

I was learning how to take a stand and take authority over my life when necessary. I also learned that even though it's taught in certain recovery groups that "once an alcoholic, always an alcoholic," this isn't true of our identity in Christ. I was learning not to accept symptoms in my body. It was a learning process that I didn't mind. I understood that, as a child of God, I didn't have to passively accept certain things anymore. As a result, I became very bold and started praying for others as well.

Redemption

The physical and emotional healing that came as a result of receiving and acting on God's Word was truly a miracle. But, He also redeemed my life in other ways as well. After my healing, it was quite evident to everyone that a monumental change had occurred in my life. People noticed how I was filling myself with the Word of God, allowing it to continue to transform me. As a result, I was asked to be a Bible study leader at my church. Not a co-leader, but a leader! The timing was perfect, and it was very redeeming for me.

I loved sharing with other women what God had done in my life. I continued to lead the studies for three years, facilitating teachings that were already written, but also incorporating my own messages. I discussed topics of healing, spiritual authority, and God's love and grace, among others. It was a beautiful time for me that helped me grow even more in the things of God as I renewed my mind with His Word.

God was training me to speak in front of people. I went from hanging my head in shame to holding it high through public speaking and teaching. It was a miracle that those who knew me got to witness before their eyes. The Lord granted me many opportunities to share my testimony from the very beginning of my healing journey. I passionately proclaimed how healing is for everyone as I told my story. Countless people thanked me for being vulnerable and for giving them hope.

No Longer an Alcoholic

As if all of these changes in my life weren't enough, God wasn't finished yet! Perhaps the greatest part of my healing is that, for the first time in my life, I was able to be around alcohol and not have a problem with it. For as long as I could remember, I was unable to attend social functions with my husband because of being in psych wards and other programs and, in general, not being well. Claude had always known me to have issues with alcohol, and even though I kept telling him I was healed, he was still skeptical, with good reason. I knew it would take time for him to see that I was truly healed and that it would last.

The first time we attended one of his functions since my healing, he still had some fear that I'd struggle with the alcohol that would be present. Shortly after arriving to the party, a bottle of champagne was opened, and a glass was put into everyone's hand, including mine. Claude glanced over at me with eyes that asked, "Are you okay?" I smiled, letting him know with facial expressions that I was more than just okay.

A toast was made, and everyone took a sip of champagne, except for Claude and me. I set my glass on a table and forgot about it. I had absolutely no issue with wanting to drink at the party, even though that night was filled with alcohol, including wine at dinner, which I had always indulged in. I simply passed it up with a smile, realizing that I had been set free. I wanted to jump up and down during the party and shout, "Jesus set me free! I am finally free from the bondage of alcohol!" I didn't say it out loud, but I screamed it to myself.

For me to be able to get through that entire night in peace and not experience temptation or torment, was nothing short of another miracle from the Lord. The peace I had knowing that I was free was overwhelming.

God's Humor

Just a couple of months after my healing, our family took a vacation to a Wisconsin water park, located on Lake Michigan. I was looking forward to it, but at the same time, I wanted to stay home. Relishing my newfound peace and safety that I was experiencing at home and with Lisa, who was mentoring me in healing and other spiritual truths, I didn't want to disturb what I was feeling.

Since the beginning of my journey of hearing God's voice, He had been placing grey feathers across my path. When I walked my dogs or went into my backyard, I'd see grey bird feathers. I finally realized that God was using them to speak to me. Sometimes I'd see them and laugh. I came to realize that God has a sense of humor, and He is a joy-filled God! He'd make me laugh through things He'd speak to me as well as through circumstances, like the feathers.

I knew that He was placing them in my path to demonstrate His presence to me. It was fun having a real relationship with the Father. It changed my world. It changed my thoughts. It changed everything! The day we left to go to Wisconsin, I was walking my dogs and saw a large grey feather in the middle of the sidewalk. Sometimes I'd pick the feathers up and collect them as precious gifts from the Lord. This time, however, I walked past it but smiled, knowing it came from my Father.

When I walked past the same location on the way home, I saw that the feather was still there on the sidewalk. I sensed the Lord prompting me to pick it up and bring it home. I wasn't sure why, but I obeyed. That afternoon, we left for Wisconsin and arrived at our hotel located on the lake's beach. We all decided to walk on the beach before heading to dinner. The joy to be on vacation and not have anxiety and anguish was such a relief! I was on cloud nine. I was thinking about my new freedom and how different my life now was, and I began praising God for all He had done.

As we walked, a wave broke on shore and washed over our feet. After the wave retreated into the lake, I glanced down and noticed a grey feather that was the exact size of the one that I had picked up in my neighborhood earlier that day. As soon as I saw it, I heard the Father say to me, "I'm with you here, too." He knew I was apprehensive to leave my home because of the peace I had. He was reassuring me that because He lived in me, He was with me everywhere I went. (I was still learning that I was one with Christ at that time.) Hearing the Father's loving, precious voice speak to me made me smile.

The following morning, I awoke at dawn, before everyone else, and snuck to the beach with a towel, my Bible, and a journal. I sat with the Lord and wrote out all of the incredible things He was saying to me. I couldn't get enough of my relationship with God. Hearing His voice and hearing Him speak to me caused a profound healing in my life. I now knew that I could go to Him for everything, and He would speak to me and guide me.

Although I was with my family, I'd still converse with my heavenly Father. Instead of being in my own world of torment while on vacation, I was in a world where I could be present with them and hear and talk to Jesus at the same time. Instead of hating life, I grew to love it and couldn't get enough of it. Instead of seeing life as a burden, I now saw it as an adventure with God. Those around me, including my husband and kids, knew something was radically different about me. I'm sure they silently wondered if my peace and joy would last, but for now, they were awestruck by the miracle they were witnessing before their very eyes.

CHAPTER 17

CONFOUNDING THE WISE

As time passed, I was able to hear from the Lord more and more each day and learned to discern which voice was His from all the other voices in and around me. One morning, as I was taking a shower, the Lord spoke to me, "You're healed now, so you can get off all of your medications." God knew that was a desire of my heart, but I was waiting for the right time to do so. Even though I'd still been taking my medications for several months since my breakthrough, I knew that eventually I would be off of them completely. And, I was convinced that I was healed, regardless of whether I was on any medication.

Even when I was taking my medications, I could still have cycles of torment, along with side effects. The fact that I could take them and experience peace only increased my conviction that I was healed. I knew I had heard God's voice and that He was assuring me that it was okay to stop taking my medications. He knew I had the revelation that I was already healed and that I wasn't getting off of the medications to prove I was healed. There is a difference.

I'm not encouraging others to stop taking medication. God's healing process is different for everyone. We all must be led by the Lord as to what is best for our individual situation.

After I showered that morning, I immediately emailed Lisa and Anita and told them what God said. I wanted to tell them in order to have accountability in my life. They knew that I was hearing from God, and they also believed that I had heard correctly and it was the right timing for me. When I learned that they supported me in my decision, I made the decision to not take another mood stabilizer, anti-depressant, anti-psychotic, or ADD medication from that day on.

I chose to wait to tell Claude until after I had been off of the medications for a while because I didn't want him to worry about me. When I finally did tell him, he was somewhat concerned and made me promise to go back on them if I ever needed to, to which I agreed. I knew I was healed, so complying with his request didn't matter to me.

What amazed him the most and convinced him of my healing was that I could sleep without any sleep medication. Initially I had trouble falling asleep as I withdrew from the sleeping pills, but after a couple of weeks, I could fall asleep within minutes, even before he did, which never happened. That proved to him the peace I was experiencing and served as the most important witness to him. Not having to take drugs twice a day and spend all that money after years of constant pills and medication changes was such a relief. I was free!

Follow-Up with Dr. Brown

After my healing, I stopped seeing my psychiatrist, Dr. Brown, because it was no longer necessary. Bipolar was not my identity anymore. After being off all medication for six months, I visited him to share the miracle that had transpired in my life. He was a Christian, so surely he'd be familiar with the Bible verses about Jesus healing the sick. I was excited to tell him my news.

To my surprise, however, when I told him what had happened, he responded by saying, "I have never heard of anyone who had been healed of bipolar disorder. There's a good chance that your symptoms will come back." Then he stared at me with a confused look that I had never seen from him.

He honestly didn't know what to do with me. He was used to people coming to talk to him about their symptoms and problems because bipolar and other mental illnesses needed to be managed on medications forever. These diseases, after all, were "incurable." I believe I was the first person to ever come into his office and declare, "I am healed and have been off of all my medications for six months. I don't have any mania or depression symptoms anymore." He was truly stunned.

The only reason I even went to see him was so he could document my healing. I had begun sharing my testimony at various Christian meetings and knew it would be powerful to have my healing recorded and verified by a doctor. But, how does a psychiatrist who doesn't believe that bipolar disorder can be healed, testify that a person who had it is healed? After his response, I knew this would be a difficult process and would take time, but I wasn't going to give up. He wouldn't document my healing, but he did verify in writing that I was no longer experiencing any symptoms at the time when he saw me.

Can't Change My Mind

Six months later, I decided to pay Dr. Brown another visit to again ask him to document my healing. He was shocked to see me, knowing that I hadn't made an appointment to see him one time in the past six months. I didn't even call him during that time, which I would frequently do during a manic episode. I reiterated to him that I was healed, and he again reminded me that bipolar disorder was incurable and that the symptoms could come back at any time.

This extremely educated, well-respected psychiatrist, with many diplomas hanging on his wall, couldn't change my mind one bit that I was healed. It didn't matter what he or anyone else said to me. No one would convince me that the bipolar disorder would come back. It was too late. I had already been living a completely different life of freedom for over a year. I had been renewing my mind with the Word of God every day and had been hearing the voice of my Father tell me that I was healed and that I could stop taking my medications. No one could take my healing from me.

The Word of God said that I was healed, and that's what I was sticking with. I threw out every book I had on bipolar disorder shortly after my healing encounter. I knew that those books were not the truth of who I was anymore. I threw out every mental illness and addiction book and even my AA Big Blue Book. I no longer needed them. Instead, I filled my library with books about healing and the Word of God, and I continued to read my Bible with new eyes.

I was never going back to my old life or old way of thinking. All those times that I had wished I could go back to my old life before my diagnoses were now gone! I had a new life, a life of relationship with God and freedom and healing. I was growing daily in my real identity and didn't want to go back to any part of my old life. I wanted to continue in my new life and move forward.

I felt like the apostle Paul when he wrote, "[13]...one thing I do: Forgetting what is behind and straining toward what is ahead, [14]I press on toward the goal to win the prize for which God has called me heavenward in Christ Jesus" (Philippians 3:13–14, NIV).

My psychiatrist again asked me questions to determine whether I had symptoms, and I responded no to every one of them. I asked him to document my healing, but he wouldn't write much except to say that I didn't have any symptoms. I was disappointed, but I knew I'd see him again. He couldn't deny what he was witnessing forever. He had even admitted to me that this was difficult for him, and he didn't know what to do about it. He was a very kind, caring man. I know that God gave him to me as a gift, realizing that I had to be under the care of a psychiatrist. I felt comfortable with him and knew that he loved the Lord and wanted to help people.

He had also told me that God must have put me in his path for a reason. I believe that God wanted him to see that people could receive the healing that was already theirs in Christ, and they could be cured of bipolar disorder, no matter what the medical books said. I know that my healing disrupted his theology. God has a way of confounding religious mindsets!

Try, Try Again

When another year had passed since I had seen Dr. Brown, I made an appointment to try once again to get him to document my healing. When I arrived, it was awkward to be back in his office, as I had become used to not going there. It had been over two years since I had been to any AA, counseling, or psychiatric visits and since I had stopped taking medication. I could tell Dr. Brown was shocked to see me when he walked into his office and found me there. I think the biggest surprise to him was that it had been two years since I had been off of the mood stabilizers and anti-depressants, which were the main medications used to manage bipolar disorder.

I immediately informed him that I was there solely to have him document my healing. He let me know that it was his last day in that office before he was transferred somewhere else where he wouldn't be able to see his previous patients. If I had not gotten in that day, I would not have a record of my healing.

I know the Lord understood that my story would be more potent with a documented note of healing from my psychiatrist. Dr. Brown asked me about my symptoms again and once again reminded me about how symptoms can come back. At the same time, I could tell he was astounded at what he was witnessing first-hand. But he was also disturbed because he wasn't sure what to make out of it. I was a new case for him, and he probably wished that I had just gone away so he wouldn't have to deal with me.

He told me he needed a little time to put something in writing and that he would send it to me. I received his letter the following week and was disappointed at what he wrote. I called him and left a voicemail for him to please call me so we could discuss it. He called back right away, and I gently confronted him, telling him that I was, in fact, healed and didn't believe that his letter was adequate to support that.

Surprisingly, he humbly admitted that he sensed the Holy Spirit was prompting him to write something different, but he didn't obey. He knew after speaking with me that he needed to follow through with what the Lord had asked him to write. This was a new experience for him, he explained. I believe he needed to be careful because he could have gotten in trouble for writing that I was healed when bipolar disorder was medically known to be incurable.

I know that he still believed that bipolar was incurable when he wrote my record, but he was also being challenged in his beliefs. I was sure that God would continue to work on his heart concerning healing. I don't know what became of Dr. Brown, but I do know that we were put into each other's lives for a reason and a season.

Below is an image of the note that Dr. Brown wrote for my record after two years of being off of my medications:

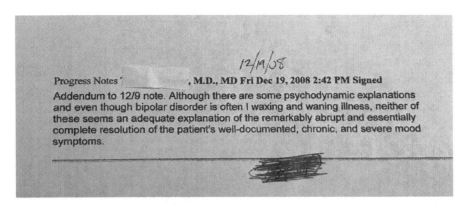

Dr. Brown's Final Evaluation

CHAPTER 18

OUR LOVING FATHER

One of the most incredible aspects of my healing and the greatest joy in my life has been coming to know God as my heavenly Father. I love to call Him my Daddy. Many of us have been through childhood pain because our earthly father didn't represent our heavenly Father to us, which I believe is God's heart for everyone. Often, we subconsciously believe that God is like our earthly father. Consequently, we may feel that He's distant, doesn't care about our needs, gets upset with us when we fail, and so forth, simply because our earthly father may have been like this.

My earthly father used fear as a tactic to get his kids to obey him. As a result, I feared punishment whenever I failed him. If I happened to say the wrong thing or if my father acted displeased with me for any reason, I feared that he would punish me. I'd immediately try to hide from him or do whatever I could to get away from him. This fear of punishment ran so deep that it manifested in anxiety that felt like sheer terror.

When I would hear others refer to God as "Father," my mind would conjure up all the negative thoughts and emotions that I held toward my earthly father, and I would project those onto God. Even though I was a Christian, if I failed at something I knew I was supposed to do—as we all do—I naturally assumed that God was mad at me, just as my earthly father would've been. Mentally and even physically, I experienced that same feeling of terror.

I always thought God was out to get me and that He would allow good opportunities to get away from me as a form of punishment. I couldn't shake the feeling that God was continually displeased with me, especially during those times when I didn't understand how to live in peace. Just as I did with my earthly father, I thought I had to earn favor with God by spending time in the Bible or going to church every week. I was always working for God's love, just as I worked for my father's love.

Through my process of healing, I have learned to see God through new eyes. Instead of having to work for God's love, I now understand that He actually pursues me with His love. He wants to draw me in and say, "I want to fill that father void in your life. Let me show you that you can trust Me with your life. I have your best interests at heart."

For those of us who have experienced abuse and trauma, being able to view God differently can be a lengthy process. But, healing begins with knowing that we have a Father who wanted us since the foundation of the world. We are His desire. He smiled the day He thought of us and hasn't stopped rejoicing over us since.

I have also come to learn that God isn't mad at me—ever! This was such a departure from how I used to think. Unlike my earthly father, God isn't upset with me and waiting to punish me when I fail. And, He's not out to get me. In fact, He's on my side, wanting the best for me. God doesn't want me to run and hide from Him when I mess up, as I did with my earthly father. He wants me to run *to* Him so He can have relationship with me and freely extend His grace to me.

Changing my old belief that I have to work to earn God's love was instrumental in my healing and a necessary first step that I had to take. Through His Word, I've learned that my behavior can never make Him love me any more or any less than He does right now, and I can never be separated from His love (Romans 8:39). There were times that I thought He truly regretted creating me, but I know now nothing could be further from the truth.

God's greatest desire for me, as with all of His children, is to experience Him and the passionate love He has for us. The more we acknowledge Him and His presence in our life, the more we'll experience His unconditional and unfailing love. And as we get to know His love, His healing will come.

The Cardinal Feather

God longs for intimacy and relationship with all of His children. He desires to speak to us in different ways, and He loves it when we realize that He's speaking to us. The following story illustrates how God once spoke to me after my healing. This type of experience is available to all of His children.

I had mentioned earlier how God was placing grey feathers in my path. When we recognize that it's God doing something, He'll do it more often. I knew the feathers were coming from

Him and that He was speaking to me through them. As a result, I kept seeing them at different times. Again, God was pursuing me with His wonderful love! He was showing me that, even though He created the entire universe, He put a feather in my path because of His love for me. He wanted me to understand that He is with me in every detail of my life. Every time I saw one, I was overwhelmed with love for my Father.

When we experience and receive His love, we will effortlessly fall deeper in love with Him. We don't have to try to muster up any kind of love; it just happens. That's what was happening in my life as I continued to discover who my Daddy truly was.

Not only did God put grey feathers in my path, but He also placed cardinals there. I began noticing them everywhere, and I even learned to recognize their voice when they sang. To this day, no matter where I travel, I can always recognize the voice of a cardinal, and Daddy will even have them appear after I hear them, just to bless me.

Sitting on my patio in the mornings, drinking coffee and spending time with my heavenly Father, within minutes, a cardinal would appear. This still happens to this day! God wanted to make sure that I wouldn't miss what He wanted to show me. One day, my neighbor, who knew nothing about these heavenly cardinal appearances, said to me, "Wow! You really have a lot of cardinals in your yard." This made me laugh! The cardinal continues to be a special gift between the Father and me.

Since God was putting grey feathers and cardinals in my path, I asked Him to allow me to find a cardinal feather. I told Him one day, "Father, before I die, I would love to find at least one cardinal feather." I had been looking for them in my yard because the birds were constantly there or flying over my house. I thought for sure that a feather would be easy to find, but that wasn't the case. I believe our Father loves it when we ask Him for things, and He loves giving us the desires of our heart.

About a year after my request, I had been praying for something big, and I needed a confirmation from the Lord. I prayed that He would confirm to me that I was making the right decision. The very next day, when I was in my backyard with my dogs, I found my very first cardinal feather. It was just lying on the grass. I had my red cardinal feather, and I knew that was the confirmation that God gave me about my decision. This was a desire of my heart, and my Father gave it to me.

To most people, that cardinal feather would mean nothing, but when you know it's a gift from your Father—the Father you always dreamed of having—it becomes a cherished gift. But the story doesn't end there. The day after finding my first cardinal feather, I found three more in the form of a triangle, again in my backyard. I sensed that they represented the Father, Son, and Holy Spirit. I was laughing with tears of joy as I picked up the feathers and added them to my collection.

I have since collected eight additional feathers at pivotal times in my life. That's our Daddy! He is the God of abundance! I asked for one cardinal feather, and He provided me with many. These feathers have become some of my most prized gifts. When God starts speaking to you in different ways, and you know that it's

Him speaking, it becomes so much fun to listen to (and "look for") His voice.

My Feather Collection from Father God

God is a joy-filled God who absolutely loves having fun with His kids. We are His children, no matter how old we are, and He wants to have fun with us. God created joy and laughter, and He is joy. Psalm 16:11 says, "In Your presence is fullness of joy" (NKJV). If you don't know Him as a God of joy and fun but you'd like to, simply ask Him to reveal Himself to you in that way. Like He did with the cardinals in my life, ask Him to show you something that will be just between you and Him that would help you know that

He's speaking to you. He's a personal and relational Father who loves revealing Himself to us in this manner!

Our Safe Place

I included the cardinal story in this chapter because it perfectly illustrates the beautiful heart of our Father toward us. I know what it's like to grow up in dysfunction and chaos; to endure verbal, physical, and sexual abuse; and to feel unlovable and as though there's something wrong with me. I know what it's like to wish that my earthly daddy could've fulfilled my needs as a little girl; but instead, he was emotionally unavailable for me. And, I know what it's like to feel unsafe.

I have compassion on both of my parents. I know in my heart that they did the best job parenting that they were capable of doing, and I've forgiven them for the harm they've done. I now understand why they had the issues they had, and I have sympathy for what they themselves endured. They were hurting people who needed a revelation of their identity in Christ.

God doesn't want us in relationships where we're continually being abused and hurt. As a teenager, I had no other choice because I had nowhere else to go. But, I've learned that God is greater than anything we could ever go through. We can get to the other side of healing and wholeness no matter what we've endured. Even though I felt unsafe as a child, God now says to me, "You are My beloved! You are safe with Me. I am your Protector."

My heavenly Father is now the one who fulfills all my needs as I depend on Him. He cherishes me, protects me, parents me, guides me, always has time for me, and loves me unconditionally, regardless of my behavior. In Him, I finally know what it's like to feel safe.

One byproduct of feeling safe in God is the disappearance of fear. The Bible teaches that God is perfect love, and perfect love casts out all fear (1 John 4:18). Understanding and believing that I am loved unconditionally by our Creator moved me from a place of fear to a place of safety. Fear is the complete opposite of love. Because I never really knew God's love for me (even though it was there all along), I continually lived in fear.

Now, as I remind myself of His love and grace toward me, fear after fear has left my life. For example, I often panicked when Claude was out of town, because I thought that someone would break into our house and kill me. I had nightmares about people chasing me and wanting to murder me. I also had dreams where I was shot, but then I'd wake up. The only way I could sleep while Claude was gone was to take a heavy dose of the sleeping pills the doctors gave me.

I was also afraid of thunderstorms, thinking that lightning would hit our house. I'd practically strangle Claude in our bed, holding on tightly and not letting go whenever there was thunder or lightning. That fear originated when I was a child, watching my mother panic during storms. We had to take shelter even if we didn't really need to because of her fear.

But, after I understood and acknowledged God's love for me, I began experiencing more and more peace — even when Claude traveled. At one point, I had stopped turning on our house alarm and completely forgot about it. It was a true miracle that, for once in my life, I actually had peace. Even during storm or tornado warnings, I no longer panic. I can walk through my house during a tornado warning without having any doubt that the Lord is protecting us, and the storm won't harm us or our home. I have noticed fear leaving various parts of my life over the years and could tell that I was literally transforming into a new person, full of God's peace.

Knowing and experiencing God's amazing love in a deeper way has been a process, and I'm still growing in it. His love is pure, unconditional, and life transforming. It's imperative for people suffering with mental illness and extreme anxiety disorders to intimately know and walk in the safe and healthy love that God has for them in order to both receive and keep their healing. There are too many forces that will continually attempt to pull us back into a life of chaos and bondage. We must daily remind ourselves of His great love for us. He will remind us too.

Our Good Shepherd

God is our Good Shepherd who continually watches over us, takes care of us, and rescues us. He wants us to live a life of rest knowing that we are in Him, which is a place of security and safety. He'll rescue us as many times as we need rescuing because He absolutely adores us.

I've always loved Psalm 23, but it came to have a very special meaning to me during my healing journey. The psalm provides a wonderful analogy of God as our Shepherd and His children as

His sheep. It was written from the perspective of a well-cared-for sheep, the shepherd boy David. He wrote this psalm with a heart of joy, ecstatic to have such a wonderful Shepherd caring for Him. David was completely dependent on His Shepherd, and as a result, experienced rest and peace and every benefit that comes from belonging to Father God.

In Psalm 23:1, David wrote, "The Lord is my best friend and my shepherd. **I always have more than enough**" (TPT, emphasis mine). Sheep are the class of livestock requiring the most attention and care. They're truly unable to take care of themselves. But, sheep are also the object of the shepherd's affection and love. A shepherd's life is devoted to taking good care of the sheep and providing for all of their needs. As a result, there's no greater reward for a shepherd than seeing his sheep satisfied, safe, and thriving under his care.

We can apply this to our heavenly Father. He loves seeing His kids flourishing and thriving. It brings Him great joy to take care of our every need, and He loves it when we depend on Him and trust in His goodness. He'll provide for us so we don't have to live a life of anxiety and worry.

For those who have grown up in chaos, turmoil, and abuse as I have, I understand that sometimes subconsciously, various triggers can emotionally transport us right back to that same unsafe place. But, under the care of the Good Shepherd, that no longer has to happen. If something tries to bring me back to my unsafe place, I remind myself that I now have a good Father who is protecting me and has my best interests at heart.

I've learned to picture my Good Shepherd watching over me to ensure that I'm safe. I imagine Him being aware of my circumstances, knowing exactly what I need every moment of every day. He's highly involved in our life because He loves us. His children are the object of His affection. We are His treasure. We belong to Him, and He delights in taking care of us. We can rest assured that in His arms we are finally safe.

The following verses confirm how much our Good Shepherd thinks about us and how loving His thoughts are toward us. As I will discuss at greater length later, part of the healing process for me has been to learn to speak and meditate on the truths of God's Word. These are just a couple of verses that I would say out loud and think on whenever possible:

"Every single moment you are thinking of me! How precious and wonderful to consider that **you cherish me constantly in your every thought!**" (Psalm 139:17, TPT, emphasis mine)

"O Lord, our God, no one can compare with you. Such wonderful works and miracles are all found with you! **And you think of us all the time with your countless expressions of love** — far exceeding our expectations!" (Psalm 40:5, TPT, emphasis mine)

I had to learn to see God as a Father who enjoys thinking about me all the time. And when He thinks about me, His thoughts are good and loving. When He thinks these good thoughts, it's never burdensome or difficult for Him. I still struggle sometimes with thinking good thoughts about others, but our heavenly Father is pure love, and He cherishes us in His every thought. It's a joy for Him to do so because He loves His children so much!

Our Place of Rest

In Psalm 23:2, I see a beautiful picture of Jesus, not only as our Good Shepherd, but also as a sheep who laid down His life for His own: "He lets me **lie down** in green pastures" (AMP, emphasis mine).

Sheep won't lie down if they're hungry and distressed. It's the shepherd's responsibility to make sure that the sheep are full, peaceful, and safe. Jesus said in John 6:35, "I am the Bread of Life. The one who comes to Me will never be hungry, and the one who believes in Me [as Savior] will never be thirsty [for that one will be sustained spiritually]" (AMP).

Throughout my journey, I've had to begin to see God as the One who satisfies my every need and provides for me in every way. I had to finally realize that God knows how to take care of me more than I know how to take care of myself. I've learned that I can "lie down" because He meets all my need (Philippians 4:19).

The reason that we're able to lie down and rest is because Jesus destroyed the works of the devil (1 John 3:8). Once I was able to understand and receive this finished work of Jesus Christ in my life, I could live in a place of rest. Rest is not passivity but a lifestyle. We can rest in our trials, we can rest in our jobs, we can rest while ministering, we can rest while parenting. Real rest comes from knowing that God sees us as forgiven, righteous, accepted, and more than conquerors. Rest comes from knowing we have a safe Shepherd who will protect us, watch over us, and provide for us.

I never understood that I was loved, accepted, and forgiven in Christ. Because of this, I always thought God was mad at me or felt like I wasn't doing enough. This caused me great anxiety instead of peace. But once I heard and received these truths for myself, I began to find rest. Just knowing that I am completely forgiven in Christ brings me great peace because I no longer have to worry about being punished for failing.

Our Good Shepherd is faithful, even when we aren't (2 Timothy 2:13). He's faithful to love us, help us, rescue us, guide us, and search for us if we wander off His path. He loves us with an everlasting love, and when we truly believe that in our heart, we will live in rest and peace.

God is so incredibly good! It will take us an eternity to discover the amazing treasures of His love and goodness. This is a huge part of our life's journey. Just as treasure hunters search out earthly wealth, our Good Father loves it when we search out His spiritual treasures in the Word and through times of intimacy with Him. There are endless attributes of His love and grace yet to be discovered, but they can be found through a relationship with our Good Shepherd. I know for myself, I'll keep seeking those eternal treasures and share about my Good Shepherd with whomever will listen.

Our Rescuer

Throughout God's Word, we see that the Lord is a rescuing God who delights in rescuing His children. For example, Psalm 23:4 tells us, "Lord, even when your path takes me through the valley of deepest darkness…you remain close to me and **lead me through it all the way**" (TPT, emphasis mine).

His ultimate rescue was delivering us out of the kingdom of darkness into the kingdom of light, the kingdom of His Son: "¹³He has rescued us completely from the tyrannical rule of darkness and has translated us into the kingdom realm of his beloved Son. ¹⁴For in the Son all our sins are cancelled and we have the release of redemption through his very blood" (Colossians 1:13–14, TPT).

And, in Luke 15:3–7, we read about Jesus leaving the ninety-nine sheep to search for the one that was lost. His entire focus was on finding that lost sheep, rescuing it, and bringing it back to His fold. What joy there is when He finds that lost sheep! I've had many times in my life where I was stressed and full of anxiety, feeling as though I wasn't going to survive whatever it was I was going through. I felt completely helpless and scared.

My healing process has taught me that if I find myself in that place again, the best thing to do is to cry out to the Shepherd for help. Dependence on the Father is the key to living a life of peace, safety, and rest, even during trials. I picture my Good Shepherd reaching out His hands and saying, "My beloved, I have come to rescue you and set you back on your feet. I will help you. I will comfort you, and you will live and not die. Rest in My loving arms and care."

When a sheep gets itself into a mess, the shepherd doesn't say, "Why did you get yourself into this mess? I can't help you! I rescued you once, but I won't do it again." Our loving Shepherd is the same way. He holds out His arms, lifts His sheep from the pit, and sets us back on our feet, saying, "Come, follow Me. I will lead you to green pastures."

For years, I was on a path of self-destruction that would eventually take my life if something didn't change. When I heard the Father say to me, "You don't have to do that anymore because My Son shed His blood for you," it was the voice of my Shepherd rescuing me. I was His lost sheep, who was self-destructing. He came searching for me when I wandered off His path.

It wasn't until years later that I understood how I didn't have to live under the influence of the kingdom of darkness any longer because Jesus' blood set me free. I began renewing my mind with the truth of who I am in Christ and God's good opinion of me.

Do you have a relational issue you're struggling with? Do you have a financial need? Do you need healing to manifest? Do you feel like you can't go on one more day? Picture the rescuing arms of your Good Shepherd coming to your aid and saving you, as you realize that Jesus is the answer to every one of your problems.

God's not mad at you or disappointed in you. Even if you made your own bed, so to speak, your Good Shepherd will come to your rescue because you are the object of His unfailing love. He will lead you back onto the right path, just as He does with a sheep who wanders.

God has walked with me on His path of healing for many years now, and it started with understanding and receiving His unconditional love. Once you realize how much God loves you, you'll also begin to view Him as your Good Shepherd, Rescuer, and Loving Father. Through the revelation of His love, you'll be able to receive, as I did, the freedom that Christ died to give you — freedom from fear, from bondage, from negative mindsets, and so much more. Never give up hope on Him rescuing you and your loved ones. What He did for me, He'll do for you!

CHAPTER 19

RECEIVING GOD'S GIFT OF RIGHTEOUSNESS

I had spent—wasted, really—my entire life being afraid of God. I was afraid of failing Him, and I was afraid of Him punishing me for my sins. I thought I had to get my behavior "right" before I could experience a relationship with Him. I never felt worthy enough to go to Him for help, and often, I'd try to hide from Him while I was in a bipolar cycle of self-injuring. This cycle led to numerous other sins, such as cussing, getting drunk, fear, anxiety, unforgiveness, bitterness, and others that I knew were opposite of my new identity in Christ. Deep down, I believed I'd never overcome all my shortcomings and get my relationship with God right.

Even after my miraculous healing, whenever I'd fail, I'd fall back into guilt and shame. I'd think, *I just received healing from the Lord, and this is how I thank Him, by continuing to fail?* I believed that I needed to be perfect, which is impossible. Only Jesus is perfect. Romans 3:23 confirms this: "For all have sinned and fall short of the glory of God" (NKJV). All means ALL. We all fail!

But, even while we were still sinners, Jesus died for us (Romans 5:8). His amazing and passionate love for us—even when we were in the midst of sinning—led Him to the cross to set us completely free. He took our sins and gave us the gift of righteousness, or right standing with Him. None of us was ever meant to live in guilt, shame, and condemnation.

Many Christians have read Romans 8:1 — "There is therefore now no condemnation to those who are in Christ Jesus" (NKJV) — but gloss over it, not realizing how impactful this verse is. I didn't fully understand this scripture for years, and even now, I'm still renewing my mind to the depths of the truths that it holds.

I used to live with so much guilt and condemnation that I was afraid to leave a store and walk out the door, thinking the alarm would go off — even though I knew I wasn't trying to steal anything! I've come to learn that God wants us to live a life of freedom. He doesn't want us to live with sin-consciousness but with righteousness-consciousness because of what Jesus did for us on the cross.

Perfect in His Sight

I mentioned in the last chapter that changing my beliefs and realizing that I didn't have to work or perform to earn God's love was a necessary first step in my healing process. I had to learn to shift from being sin-conscious, where I was always focused on doing something wrong, to being righteousness-conscious, where I was focused on God's grace toward me. Being righteousness-conscious is simply seeing ourselves as God sees us, and not seeing ourselves trapped in the bondage of old sin habits.

When the Lord spoke to me while I was cutting my arm and watching the blood flow, it was a powerful life-changing moment. But, it took years before I understood more completely what He meant by it. He was trying to tell me that I was righteous in His sight, or had right standing with Him—regardless of what I did or didn't do.

We become righteous by faith in Jesus Christ—and nothing else. It's that simple! The gift of right standing means that when God looks at us, He sees us as flawless in Christ. He sees no sin in us. He doesn't view us with sin or failures because of the shed blood of Christ. We stand before Him perfect in His sight.

This is His gift to us because of His love for us. It took me awhile to learn that there was nothing I could do to earn this gift, because Jesus has already done everything. My part was to receive His gift by faith in Jesus. God was trying to tell me that day when I was cutting that I didn't have to punish myself for my sins because Jesus took all of my sin upon Himself at the cross. At the same time, He freely gave me the gift of right standing. Jesus has done this for every person on earth (1 John 2:2). He took all the sins of the entire world upon Himself, and exchanged them for the gift of right standing when He sacrificed Himself at Calvary.

God continually pursued me with His love and grace and wanted to get my attention to tell me, "My beloved, you are right with Me. Come to Me to help you overcome all of your struggles. Draw on My life inside of you to meet all your needs. You don't have to wait until you clean yourself up; I've already made you clean and holy and pure and righteous with My shed blood. You can't add anything by your behavior. Your behavior does not affect how I see you." He's saying the same thing to you today.

In the book *Classic Christianity*, author Bob George gives an example that has helped me better understand God's gift of righteousness. George explains that when people can jelly, fruit, or vegetables, the jars must first be sterilized before they can be filled. After the jars are filled, their lids are then sealed so no contaminates can enter the jars. In the same way, Jesus purged us of our sins and cleansed us so He could live in us, sealing us with the Holy Spirit (Ephesians 1:13).

Reading this made me want to get up and dance! I realized that I never again had to hide from the Lord. Knowing that I'm in right standing with Him helps me say, "No!" to the voices of condemnation, guilt, and shame that still try to speak to me. I've learned through my journey that righteousness isn't only an amazing gift; it's also a weapon against the enemy's lies and accusations.

What Sin?

In Revelation 12:10, our enemy is called "the accuser" because he attempts to continuously accuse us by reminding us how we've failed or how we're less than perfect. God, however, focuses on what is right with us. He doesn't point out our sins and our failures. In fact, because of the blood of Jesus, God says, "Their sins and lawless acts I will remember no more" (Hebrews 10:17, NIV).

One day, my friend Lisa shared this nearly unbelievable truth with me from God's Word. As we talked about righteousness and how I felt as though I kept falling short due to my sins, she asked me, "Do you know that your past, present, and even future sins have already been forgiven by faith in Jesus?" I told her that I needed to see this for myself in the Word before I believed it, as it sounded too good to be true.

Sure enough, there it was in Hebrews 8:12—"For I will forgive their wickedness and will remember their sins no more" (NIV). (See also Psalm 103:3; Isaiah 1:18; Romans 5:18; and others.) I immediately realized that I had been duped again by listening to lies and error and even wrong teaching.

This revelation led me down a path of discovering the truth about our righteousness in Christ. What I found is that righteousness is discussed throughout the New Testament because we now live in the new covenant era. God made an unbreakable covenant with us, and we get to receive and enjoy the benefits of it by putting our faith in His Son.

As born-again believers, we're part of the new covenant because we're in Christ. We're safe and secure in Him. Even when we fail (which we will), it doesn't change our position in the new covenant. All of God's blessings are now ours, and there's nothing we can do to earn them. We don't have to be good enough. We don't have to try and twist God's arm. God is a giver, and He loves giving to His children. All we have to do is receive what He has already so freely given, including His forgiveness of our sin.

We have a heavenly Daddy, a Father that we don't ever have to hide from. He is waiting and longing for a relationship with us, His beloved children. We don't have to "get it right" to experience

Him or hear from Him. He views us as flawless, perfect, and beautiful in Christ. No one can take the special place that we have in our Father's heart.

I've finally learned how to rest in God's love and grace, knowing that He's not mad at me, but rather madly in love with me! I've come to understand that God wants me to be more preoccupied with a relationship with Him than with sin. He wants me to have a righteousness-consciousness instead of a sin-consciousness. The fruit of me knowing my right standing with God has been right living or holiness. When I finally believed and accepted that I'm righteous, worthy, and free in Christ, my behavior began to conform to His will for my life. Only when I was finally set free of condemnation by believing what His Word says about me did I become free to follow Him with all my heart.

Giving Myself Grace

When we live knowing that we're completely forgiven, accepted and loved, it helps us extend grace to ourselves when we fail. One of the greatest challenges that most of us face, including me, is learning to love ourselves despite our messes and failures. God wants us to learn to love the people that He created us to be, and He wants us to know that, although we're righteous in Him, we'll still fail. But when we do, it'll never change our position of right standing, and it won't change the way He sees us. His love for us is constant and consistent, and it never fails.

As I began to walk more and more in this truth, I also learned that it was then up to me to reject any wrong thinking that told me God was upset with me or loves me less because of my failure. His desire is for us to come boldly to Him in the midst of our failure so He can help us. Hebrews 4:16 instructs us, "…let us come boldly to the throne of our gracious God. There we will receive his mercy, and we will find grace to help us when we need it most" (NLT). He wants to shower us with His grace!

I know for myself, if I believe that a person is mad at me, I'll tend to avoid that person. Sometimes we subconsciously do that with God, which is what I did for many years. But He doesn't want us to hide from Him. He knows that He alone is our answer, our healing, our peace, our joy, and our help in time of need.

It was so freeing to realize that my heavenly Father doesn't expect me to be perfect. As Christians, we're only perfect in our spirit (where the Holy Spirit resides), but our behavior will never be perfect. Yet, the more we grow in knowing who we are in Him and how much we're loved by Him, the less sin will appeal to us, and we won't desire it. I don't like it when I sin because it goes against who I am in Christ. But when I do sin, I'm learning to stand against the voices of accusation that tell me how I messed up. Instead, I give myself grace, just as the Lord gives me grace.

When I fail, I go to my Father and tell Him I'm sorry, because we're in relationship, and I allow Him to love me and show me how to have victory in my struggle. Jesus took all of my condemnation, and that means I no longer have to live a life of beating myself up. I've learned how to extend grace to myself, which I never knew how to do before receiving my healing.

We all need to learn how to show ourselves love, compassion, and grace. I'm not where I want to be yet in this area, but I've left where I used to be. Chances are, you have too. If not, you can choose to do so at this very moment. Tell yourself, "I am loved. I am safe with my Father. He has compassion on me and doesn't love me any less when I fail. My Father forgives me and wants to help me. I am flawless and beautiful in Christ."

I find it calming and soothing to remind myself of these truths from God's Word. When I do, I envision my heavenly Father speaking directly to me as His precious beloved child to help me remember that I'm loved and safe, no matter what. Here are two scriptures I use to remind me of how God feels about me:

"You're beautiful from head to toe, my dear love, beautiful beyond compare, absolutely flawless." (Song of Songs 4:7, MSG)

"I've never quit loving you and never will. Expect love, love, and more love!" (Jeremiah 31:3, MSG)

Grace for My Parenting Mistakes

Perhaps no one knows better than I do how it feels to muddle through the mire of guilt produced by years of parenting mistakes and failures. Like me, you may also believe that you were far from a perfect parent. I'd like to share some news with you: There's no such thing as a perfect parent. Our heavenly Father is the only perfect parent there has ever been or will ever be.

Part of my healing process was learning to forgive myself for my past parenting mistakes. We can bring our parenting failures to our Father and allow Him to heal our heart. He realizes the pain that some of us have endured, which caused us to behave in ways that failed our children. But, there's no mistake or failure that hasn't been conquered by Jesus' death on the cross.

If you're like me and made your share of parenting mistakes, I encourage you to do what I did: As a symbol of releasing guilt and pain, hold your hands out to Him, and give Him all of the burdens that you've been carrying. Envision any failures you've had upon the body of Jesus hanging on the cross. His broken body absorbed every mistake we have or ever will make. He wants us to let these failures go so we can be free.

I had to come to the realization that God loves my children more than I ever could. He longs for all of us to give our children to Him. If you have kids who are in bondage to addictions or are making wrong choices and they don't want help, give them to Jesus. It may take time to see change in certain situations, but never give up hope. Jesus will pursue them with His love through people who He'll strategically place in their lives.

Throughout my addiction and bondage, I kept believing that I would one day become a better parent to my kids. I tried so hard to be the best parent possible, and there were moments when I did succeed at parenting. However, like all of us, I also failed at times. Some of us have to overcome more than others, especially if we were raised in a dysfunctional environment, but I did the best I could.

God doesn't just heal bodies and hearts; He also heals families. He's healed my family in many ways, and I'm happy to report that my children are all doing well, despite my parenting deficiencies. They've gone through trials, but they too are learning that God is good, and He helps them no matter what they face. It's important for us to shed our parenting guilt and stop blaming ourselves for the mistakes our children make. Turn them over to the Lord, and watch Him go to work in their lives.

As part of my healing process, one day I apologized to all of my kids for failing them at times while they were growing up. I explained that I didn't have a real parent role model, and I did the best I could with what I knew. They appreciated me taking time to do this and even said, "You don't need to apologize; we turned out great!" As parents, we should humble ourselves and tell our children that we're sorry we failed them. This is a gift we can give them that opens the door for forgiveness if they're harboring any unforgiveness toward us.

I never received an apology from my parents or stepparents during my childhood, even though I desperately wanted and needed one. But, I later received one from my heavenly Father on their behalf. I'd like to share this apology and encourage you to receive it for yourself, believing that your Father is saying these very words to you right now:

"My precious child, I want you to know that it hurt My heart to see the pain that you've gone through in your life. It grieved Me that you didn't feel safe. It grieved My heart to see the abuse you endured, and it hurt My heart that you weren't treated like a dearly loved child, because that was My desire for you. I want you to know that the verbal, physical, emotional, and sexual abuse that you endured was never My heart for you.

"Precious one, today is a new day. If you're still struggling with pain and trauma, give it to Me. Let Me heal your broken heart. Let Me put it back together again and make it new. You're an overcomer in Me. It's time to leave all of that mess behind you and focus on Me and all of the good things that I have planned for you in your journey. Leave the regret of the past at the cross. It's time to move on. You're a new creation in Me, and I see you as blameless and flawless in My sight because of the blood of Christ. I want you to start viewing yourself the way that I see you. You're precious, special, unique, and loved. You matter!

"I'll keep reminding you of these truths until they sink deep down, and your heart is fully persuaded. Let Me parent you the way that you were supposed to be parented. Let Me show you that I'm now your perfect, heavenly Father, and I will love you and care for you the way that you were supposed to be loved and cared for. I love you, My sweet child! You can never be separated from My love, and I want you to know that I'll never be disappointed in you. Thank you for being My child. You bring My heart so much joy just by being My child."

CHAPTER 20

LEARNING TO THINK AND SPEAK VICTORIOUSLY

When people grow up with trauma, abuse, dysfunction, and emotionally unavailable parents, it takes time to stop viewing life through the lens of rejection, shame, and condemnation and begin seeing it through our real identity in Christ. The first step to being able to do this is by adhering to Romans 12:2 —

"And do not be conformed to this world [any longer with its superficial values and customs], but be transformed *and* progressively changed [as you mature spiritually] by the renewing of your mind [focusing on godly values and ethical attitudes], so that you may prove [for yourselves] what the will of God is, that which is good and acceptable and perfect [in His plan and purpose for you]" (AMP).

The word *progressively* in this verse means, "making progress toward better conditions" (Dictionary.com). In other words, renewing our mind is a process and not something that happens instantly. We're all on a journey to change the way we think in order to experience "better conditions," which to me is receiving everything that Jesus died to give us — our incredible inheritance as children of God.

For years, my identity was a bipolar, borderline, alcoholic. I had to learn to shift from seeing myself with those labels to seeing myself as a child of God. This is my new identity. But, just because I now identify as a child of God, it doesn't mean that I never have instances of mistaken identity. I may react out of frustration or impatience and yell at my kids or get mad at the driver who cuts me off. Or, I may allow myself to fall into discouragement or beat myself up with guilt. These are all cases of mistaken identity because during these times I forget that I'm loved, forgiven, righteous, beautiful, and victorious in Jesus.

It's so important, not only for myself, but as an example for others as well, to continuously renew my mind with good teachings that focus on my true identity in Christ. I need to remind myself that I am complete in Christ, a new creation, and have been healed by the stripes of Jesus.

These truths from God's Word are reality, whether they're coming to pass in my life at a particular moment or not. For all of us, what gets in the way of God's promises manifesting in our life is the way we think. Proverbs 23:7 tells us that as a man "thinks in his heart, so is he" (NKJV). This is why we must change the way we think in order to believe the beautiful love letter God has written to us, which is His Word.

Some beliefs can change in an instant, like the moment I knew I was healed. Many times, however, changing our beliefs is a process that takes time. By focusing on God's promises, I've learned that I don't have to let my past control me, and I can be an overcomer in Christ instead of a victim. But to do so, I had to turn from a lifetime of negative mindsets that were established in my childhood to thinking like the new creation that I've become in Christ.

There were areas in my life where I was able to quickly renew my mind to God's truth, but other places took longer. And, there are some areas where my mind is still being renewed. Again, I've had to give myself grace for this journey, and so will you. It may not happen overnight, but as we continue in God's Word, it will happen.

John 8:32 says, "…you will know the truth, and the truth will set you free" (NIV). If truth sets us free, then believing lies about God and about ourselves will keep us in bondage. I used to believe a lot of lies about God and myself, and I had no idea who I was in Christ. This is why I stayed stuck in my cycles of negativity for so long.

The following examples from my life help depict the importance of changing our thinking. I've experienced major spiritual growth since my miraculous healing, but it's because I've taken the time to renew my mind to the love of God and my righteousness in Christ. Years of planting the seeds of God's Word in my heart and mind have resulted in a harvest of peace and joy. You can do this as well. Allow these stories to encourage and inspire you to begin planting God's Word in your heart today.

Learning to Trust

As I've discussed, I grew up with four parents whom I never trusted. I experienced abuse, abandonment, and neglect. The core struggle I've had my entire life is a fear of rejection and abandonment. I've come a long way in this area, but at times, I still need to remind myself of God's truth and change the negative thoughts that attempt to infiltrate my mind.

Because of my childhood chaos, I became adept at watching every move of those around me. It was a survival technique I learned at a very early age. I carefully examined my stepfather to determine what mood he was in so I could emotionally prepare myself and watch what I said around him. I also needed to be aware in case my father was high on drugs. Sometimes I just stayed out of the way and isolated myself in my room for my own protection.

Knowing the atmosphere of whichever home I was in and the moods of those near me helped me know how to behave so I wouldn't get in trouble. I've learned, however, that while this helped me survive my childhood, it doesn't work in adult relationships. As an adult, I've had to learn to not view everyone and every situation through a lens of rejection and distrust. I've also had to learn to trust the people that God has put into my path to help me.

Although I've come a long way, I haven't completely conquered all the negative feelings and thoughts that can bombard me from time to time. For example, recently a friend of mine posted some statuses on Facebook that I believed were directed at me. I was convinced that she was upset with me and was rejecting me. I found out later that she was referring to some personal things that had just happened in her life that had absolutely nothing to do with me. But, not initially knowing this, I allowed my mind to tell me that she was rejecting me.

One thing I now understand as a result of knowing who I am in Christ, is that even if someone does reject me, it's not a reflection of who I am. That person's rejection doesn't take away my worth and value. And, if I am rejected, I believe that it would happen *for* me, not *to* me. There are times when people are in our life only for a season, and we need to be sensitive to what the Lord is doing through them.

I have learned over the last twelve years that my good Father will never leave me, no matter who may reject me. In the past, if someone rejected me or I had perceived rejection that never became a reality, it could literally lead me to the psych ward. I would meditate on those lies of rejection and continue to get discouraged and depressed, which would result in thoughts of abandonment.

I know now, though, that most of the time when thoughts of rejection come, they're not true. They're not reality. I'm also learning not to be so sensitive if people don't react the way I would or the way I'd want them to. Just because people don't like your Facebook post or return your call or text right away, it doesn't mean they're upset with you or rejecting you. Sometimes people have bad days and are dealing with things that have nothing to do with you.

These are the issues I've had to walk through in my everyday life, and in doing so, I've realized that there are trustworthy people who have a solid foundation of their identity in Christ. I've also learned to love people in their messes. We're all in the process of renewing our minds with truth. We may struggle with something that another person has victory in, while we may have victory in an area where that person struggles. It's important to give each other love and grace and keep channels of communication open.

The Lord is helping me to maintain peace in relationships and is taking away the fear of rejection that had caused so much torment in my life. Isaiah 26:3 tells us that we will have perfect peace when our mind is focused on God. When thoughts of rejection try to pierce my heart, I do my best to keep my eyes on Jesus. He leads me and guides me in all my relationships, including knowing what to say or not to say.

When I believed that I was unworthy of love, I lived that out in my life. I just assumed that people would reject me, and it caused me to isolate myself. It also resulted in me guarding my heart and not trusting anyone or backing away from people because of possible abandonment. Once I was persuaded in my heart that I'm loved and accepted, I began to live that out in my life instead, and the fruit of that has been healthy relationships and learning how to let go of toxic ones. It all started with my heart and believing what God said about me in His Word. Our good Father will help you as well.

God showed me that when we truly understand that we're worthy of others' love after receiving His love, we'll find peace in our relationships. I was amazed that relationships could actually give me joy instead of worry and torment. God wants us to rest in His love and in the finished work of Jesus and experience His perfect peace. If I can do this, so can you. You can change the way you think, and you can live in peace.

Our Powerful Words

It didn't take me long after my healing to understand how powerful my thoughts and beliefs are. They have literally determined the direction that my life has taken. I've already discussed how, when we truly believe that God is good, that He loves and accepts us, and that we are more than conquerors through Him, we'll live out those beliefs from the heart in the form of joy, peace, and freedom. But there's also another reason why our beliefs are so important, and that's because what we believe will ultimately affect our speech. Consider the following scriptures:

"And since we have the same spirit of faith, according to what is written, 'I believed and therefore I spoke,' we also believe and therefore speak." (2 Corinthians 4:13, NKJV)

"What you say flows from what is in your heart." (Luke 6:45, NLT)

Once I realized that I was loved and accepted and that the Father had only beautiful thoughts toward me, I began to speak from a heart that was full of love and acceptance. I grew up with a negative, pessimistic mindset; therefore, most of my speech was negative. And, I spoke death over myself while I was in bondage. The fruit of all of that negativity and death was continual torment and lack of peace.

Part of my healing journey over the past twelve years has been to change both the way I think and the way I speak. I no longer speak death over myself. Now, I speak God's Word over situations instead of expecting worst-case scenarios. Every year that goes by, I see progress in this area. I'm learning to speak as my Father speaks, which I've discovered is a much better way to live!

Again, if you're not where you want to be in this area, give yourself grace. There are times when we mess up and say things we regret, but instead of dwelling on our failures, we can choose to move forward. It may take time to completely break free from a lifetime of negativity, but it's possible to do. All it takes is a desire and asking Jesus for help.

The following story is a great example of speaking life over our situations. Last year, my landscaper planted two burning bushes in my front yard. After a couple of months, he came back to weed my yard and told me that one of my burning bushes was almost dead. He removed it and left it by my garbage can with its roots exposed. I loved that bush and was saddened by this news.

After looking at it for a couple of days, I decided to replant it because I didn't want to give up on it. I watered it and spoke life over it, decreeing that it would live and not die! I did this for several weeks, every time I walked past it. Then winter came, and I forgot about it. My landscaper, who is a Christian, knew what I did, but he had his doubts at the time that it would work.

Well, just today he came to my house to weed and noticed the bush. He was shocked at how well it's doing. It's now thriving! Also, the other bush that was planted at the same time has been half eaten by rabbits, but the one I spoke life to has not been touched by the rabbits. I'm ecstatic! This boosted my faith and helped me realize even more how powerful our words are.

Proverbs 18:21 says, "Death and life are in the power of the tongue" (KJV). Imagine the profound effects of speaking life over ourselves and our situations. Our words have more power and authority than we know. God spoke the entire universe into existence. He gave us mouths to speak so we can speak His words of love and life into ourselves and the world around us.

If you're tempted to speak negative words and words of death as I used to be, I encourage you to change your speech. Speak life over those around you and over situations that appear dead, and watch the Lord perform resurrections right before your eyes!

To help me learn to speak life, I began meditating on and speaking the declarations below. I found these to be a good place to start speaking God's Word over myself, telling myself who I am in Christ and what belongs to me. I encourage you to say these statements out loud as often as you need to, believing in your heart that they'll change you from the inside out.

"I can do anything because Jesus, who lives in me, gives me the strength." (Philippians 4:13; Colossians 3:3)

"I have the light of Jesus in me for all to see." (Matthew 5:14)

"I am victorious because of Jesus." (Romans 8:37)

"I am loved and nothing can separate me from God's love." (Romans 8:38–39)

"I am forgiven." (Psalm 103:3; Colossians 2:13; Hebrews 8:12)

"I am protected by my heavenly Father." (Psalm 91)

"My heavenly Father is always on my side, so I don't need to be afraid of anyone." (Psalm 118:6–7; Romans 8:31–32)

"I have all authority over the enemy because Jesus defeated him and because I am a child of God." (Luke 10:19; 1 John 4:4)

"I am complete in Christ." (Colossians 2:10)

The Bible tells us in 2 Peter 1:3 that God's divine power has given us everything we need for life and godliness *through the knowledge of Him*. This means that we have everything we will ever need in His Word! It's entirely up to us, however, to choose to use these tools to help us escape our past, our bondages, and our weaknesses. Whether it's emotional or physical, healing can sometimes be a process, but the sooner we learn what God says about us, believe it, and speak it, the sooner our healing will come.

One thing I've learned through my healing journey is that we never know when trials and attacks are going to come, so we always need to be ready. Had I not been renewing my mind to God's Word and practicing watching my words, I would not have been prepared for the battle that lay ahead.

CHAPTER 21

READY OR NOT

Claude has been very athletic his entire life, and he doesn't drink or smoke. Yet, at age forty-six, he started having chest pains for a couple of weeks. His doctor ordered tests, and when they came back, Claude was instructed to get an angiogram to detect any blockages in his heart.

Hearing this news, the talons of fear tried their best to grip me. Because of my past trauma, my first thought is often to expect the worst, but I now recognize that and refuse to stay in that place. I now remind myself that everything is going to be okay, which is my way of combating negative thoughts and emotions. So when fear attacked, I fought back by declaring, "Lord, I trust You in this, no matter what happens."

I've discovered that fear and other negativity won't always leave us right away. I had to regularly speak God's truth out loud and to myself to remain in a place of peace during this trial. Romans 10:17 tells us that our faith grows when we hear God's Word, so when we hear ourselves speak His truth over and over, we eventually believe it in our heart. It's always tempting to give up or get lax in fighting this faith fight, but there are times when we cannot afford to do so. For me, this was definitely one of those times.

The doctors told us that Claude would need a couple of stents inserted to open up his arteries if they were blocked, which would mean staying in the hospital overnight. The day of the procedure, anxiety was weighing heavily on my husband. The nurse who was assigned to us began saying a beautiful Spirit-filled prayer over him. God used her to shower my husband with His love and peace. I didn't even have time to pray because she just jumped in! It's so comforting to know that God is aware of our battles, and He's with us through them all. I'm certain that He ordained for this nurse to be assigned to Claude as His gift to us.

Claude was then taken from the room we were in to have his procedure done. A little while later, I checked the time and realized that the procedure should be nearly finished. Just then, the same nurse arrived in my room with a serious look on her face. She took a seat next to me and gently held my hand while relaying the news: "Your husband needs bypass surgery. He could need triple or even quadruple bypass surgery."

Here I was thinking he would just need a stent or two, only to find out that Claude, who is scared of blood and medical procedures, required open heart surgery—one of the most difficult surgeries to endure. I stared blankly at the nurse, in complete shock.

Choosing Peace

The nurse said a reassuring prayer for me before the doctor entered the room. The surgeon, also a Christian, was interrupted by a phone call as he was speaking to us, revealing the ringtone of a Christian song. I believe that God allowed me to hear that ringtone, knowing it would give me peace and assure me that He would be guiding the surgeon's hands. Before we had time to process what was happening, we learned that Claude's triple bypass surgery would be two days later.

My world changed in an instant, and I suddenly had a choice: I could maintain my peace and trust the Lord, or I could go back to insanity. I knew God was working in our situation and actually was extremely grateful that He was using this trial to save Claude's life. If he had not gone to the doctor, they said he would've dropped dead of a heart attack. The choice was mine, and I decided I must stay in peace at all costs.

I stayed with Claude as much as possible, but I also had to be at home for my kids. Because of all that Jesus had done for me over the past several years, I was able to be a source of strength for Claude, helping to ease his fears. In the past, I would've fallen apart in front of him, which would've only made matters worse. I knew that I had to stay strong for my family, and by God's grace, I could do so through the strength of Christ. Claude had been there for me in my time of need, and now it was my turn to support him.

Two days later, our entire family had gathered around Claude in his hospital room. We all held hands as he said a prayer for us. He wanted to demonstrate to our children that His trust was in the Lord. My friend Lisa also came to be with me that day, and we spent the day praying and talking.

At one point, I realized that the nurse didn't call me back at the time she said she would. She had initially told me that Claude's heart had been stopped by the doctors, and he was hooked up to a machine that circulated his blood throughout his body. She had promised to call me once he was off the machine, after the bypasses were attached, and his heart was beating on its own, which she said would be in about an hour.

Since well over an hour had passed and I still hadn't heard from her, fear attacked once again with a series of rapid-fire worst-case scenarios: *What if he didn't make it? What if there's a problem? How I am going to face my kids?* I couldn't afford to allow these thoughts to infiltrate my mind. I knew I'd have to take a strong stand against them because they weren't going to go away by themselves. Again, I had a choice of how to respond to the onslaught of fear.

I told Lisa what was happening, and she and I prayed, invoking the promises of God. After experiencing God's love and goodness in the years after my healing, I knew I could trust Him throughout this entire process. After praying, the peace of God replaced fear in my heart. Then, finally, after two and a half hours, the nurse called to tell me that Claude's surgery was successful.

Hopeless No More

After Claude awoke, I nervously made my way into the recovery room. Seeing my normally strong, independent husband attached to so many tubes and machines was difficult for me. When I saw him lying there, completely helpless, my mind suddenly flashed back to when he came into our bedroom after one of my many relapses and found me helpless and out of control, bathed in blood.

I knew at the time that he was terrified seeing me in that condition, but until I stood by his bedside on this day, I couldn't personally relate to the emotions that he must've had to wrestle with. I've experienced plenty of hopelessness, anxiety, and fear, but always for myself; not for someone I love. This was very different and unsettling for me.

I now understood how utterly hopeless Claude felt for me—for us. I, too, had believed that my condition was completely hopeless. But now I know that through Jesus, we never have to feel hopeless again. In my own strength, there wasn't much I could do for Claude as he lay there hooked up to breathing tubes. But, praise God, I no longer operate out of my own strength!

I now have someone greater to turn to for help. Through faith in Christ's finished work, I knew that God would get us through this harrowing experience. Unlike before my healing, when I never knew what the next day would bring, or even if there would be a next day, I can now look to tomorrow with great hope and expectation. And that's exactly what I chose—and still daily choose—to do.

FINAL THOUGHTS

I shared the story of Claude's health scare because I want to demonstrate how far God has brought me since reading Anita's life-changing email in the Walmart parking lot twelve years ago. If Claude's episode had happened before my healing, or even in the first few years after my healing, I would not have been much help to him at all. In fact, I probably would've completely fallen apart.

I've learned so much about the Lord and His great love for me throughout my healing journey, I now feel as though I can conquer anything. And I can, because I am more than a conqueror through Christ (Romans 8:37). I'm so grateful to Jesus for setting me free!

Through this book, I hope to encourage others that God can get them to the other side of freedom in Him no matter where they are right now or where they've been. When we depend on Him and believe the precious promises in His Word, we can all live as victorious conquerors instead of victims.

There are times when we must trust God literally one day—even one moment—at a time. But I've learned that no matter what circumstance I'm facing, I have a God who is bigger than any problem or battle that comes my way. He's always with us, and He'll guide us through every step.

My Whole New World

Earlier in the book, I told the story of how my family went to Disney World right after I had gone to rehab for alcoholism. We rode the ride It's a Small World, and I had continuous mental torment throughout the ride. I was on vacation in one of the happiest places on earth, yet my mind was bombarded with thoughts of relapsing on alcohol and even killing myself.

In my tenth year of healing, after our kids were grown, we all went back to Disney World. In fact, we returned while I was in the process of writing this book. I was so excited to see the park with new eyes and to go back on It's a Small World because I've changed so much since the last time I was on it.

As soon as we got on the ride, I realized I had a big smile on my face. I thanked God for my freedom and healing. I thoroughly enjoyed the ride, grateful for my family and my new life. Instead of hearing the voices of torment, I heard the voice of love, saying to me, "I am so proud of you. I love you. I enjoy seeing you walk in the healing that was My gift to you." I heard the encouraging, loving voice of my Father instead of the voice of condemnation, shame, and guilt.

After the ride, my family and I decided to see an animated show. While watching the show, which I have done countless times in our many trips to Disney World, I saw something with new eyes, and my Father spoke to me. There was a clip of the movie *Aladdin*, where one of the characters was riding on a carpet. The song "A Whole New World" played during the movie clip. As I listened to the song, the Lord told me that He has brought me into a WHOLE new world.

And, He's right. He's brought me into a world of healing and wholeness. I have gone from a place of torment to a whole new world of peace, joy, and freedom! God has given me a brand-new life through Jesus — a life that's available to everyone. We *all* qualify because of Jesus. We don't have to earn healing; it's a gift.

The Healing Process

No matter where you are in your life, you can move from a place of trauma, depression, anxiety, and fear to a whole new world in Christ. Even for those reading this who may have severe mental illness, you can be free and walk in healing and wholeness, regardless of the diagnoses or labels you've been given.

Getting to know and experience God as a good Father through the truths in the Bible, listening to teachings on God's grace and healing, and hearing the Lord speak loving words to my heart has provided the greatest healing in my life and has allowed me to stay free.

Staying healed and free from bondage is as important as receiving healing in the first place. I understand why many people can't get free or maintain their freedom if they do. I believe that I could choose to return to being bipolar anytime I want. That's because negative, anxiety-filled thoughts still come to me. I have to purposely stand against thoughts of disappointment, rejection, loneliness, abandonment, failure, and so forth.

I have to turn to the Word of God, meditate on truths that are contrary to those negative thoughts, allow Jesus to love me and speak His words to me, and use my authority when necessary to negate those thoughts.

What I'm describing isn't a formula or a magic wand. It's a process and a new way of living. Right now, for example, God is placing volunteers and others to help me with the huge vision He's given me for my ministry center. I've had overwhelming thoughts during this time that want me to believe I'm all alone and won't succeed in making this vision a reality. These thoughts were designed to make me quit what God has called me to do.

I recognize that these are thoughts from the enemy, and it's up to me to choose to ignore them and not believe them. Instead, I turn to my Father who reminds me that He's helping me, providing for me, and working behind the scenes on my behalf.

Jesus died so that you and I can be whole, healed, and set free — body, soul, and spirit. Isaiah 61:1 reads, "The Spirit of the Sovereign LORD is on me, because the LORD has anointed me to proclaim good news to the poor. He has sent me to bind up the brokenhearted, to proclaim freedom for the captives and release from darkness for the prisoners" (NIV).

The original Hebrew word for *bind up* means to "bandage a wound, give relief, put on a compress" (*Strong's Exhaustive Concordance of the Bible*, Hebrew Dictionary #2280, s.v. "chabash"). We need to imagine Jesus taking our pain or brokenness, bandaging it up, and making it healed and whole again.

When a wound is bandaged, it takes time to heal. In the same way, it takes time to renew our minds with God's truth that will set us free and heal the negative heart messages that over time have caused us to feel brokenhearted.

Jesus already provided this healing for us at the cross. He took our pains and our sorrows (Isaiah 53:5) and gave us a brand-new heart. We just have to receive what He did for us and believe it so we can live it out in our lives.

God's Love Letter to You

Several years ago, God gave me a vision to encourage me with my broken heart. I trust that His words will help you as well. I wrote it here as an excerpt from my book, *122 Love Letters from the Throne of Grace.*

"...I saw a picture of a heart lying on the ground. The heart was being kicked. The heart was being stabbed. The heart was being beaten. All of this symbolized some of the pain my heart has felt during my lifetime. Then, I saw Jesus pick up the battered, lifeless heart in His hands. He carefully picked the heart up and kissed it. He caressed it ever so gently. He wiped off all of the dirt. Next, I saw that the heart looked brand new with no wounds on it. He placed the new heart back inside of me to symbolize that His love is what will heal all of the rejection wounds I have had in my life.

"Next, I heard Him say, 'My beloved child, it saddens Me to see the pain you have been through in your life. Rejection from others was never a part of My plan, and I see how it has wounded your heart. I see how you are

afraid to share your heart with others. I see how you have fear of being vulnerable with others for fear of being hurt. Precious one, I want you to know that you can always be vulnerable with Me, and I will never, ever reject you. I will never, no never, break your heart!

"'I want you to share your pain, your concerns, your cares, and your worries with Me. I don't want you to ever be afraid to share what is on your heart with Me. Ever! Nothing will ever change the way I feel about you, no nothing! You will always be My beloved, precious child. …Let Me heal all of the sadness and brokenness you have been through. Let Me take away your fear of rejection. Give it to Me, and I will set it at the foot of the cross because that is where it belongs. My Son carried all of your sorrows at the cross.

"'…Let Me do a deep inner healing in your heart and soul. Let Me take that battered heart and make it new. Let Me kiss it with My love. I care deeply about you. Rest assured, I will never, ever break your heart or hurt you. You can trust Me, My beloved.'"

Can you hear the Father speaking these words to you now? Know that He always has your best interests in mind. If you ask Him, He'll reveal to you any lies you may've fallen for that are preventing you from receiving from Him. He wants to break off those lies and set you free with His love and truth.

Believe in the Lord's goodness and love toward you. Walk in His grace. And, never stop holding on to the hope for the healing that is yours through Jesus Christ.

PRAYER OF SALVATION

Heavenly Father, I believe that Jesus Christ is Your Son and that He took my place and died for my sins. I believe that on the third day, He was raised from the dead so that I could have eternal life and right standing with You. Thank You, Jesus, for taking my punishment for sin and making peace with the Father on my behalf. At this very moment, I choose to make Jesus the Savior and Lord of my life. I repent (change my mind) and turn from my past into a new future with You. I go forward now as Your child, with You as my Father, and with heaven as my home.

According to Your Word in Romans 10:9–10, I am now born again. I am a new creation in Christ (2 Corinthians 5:17). Thank You for viewing me as if I never sinned. Nothing can remove me from this place of right standing with You. Thank You that Your life is in me at this very moment, and Your Holy Spirit will continue to work out victory in every area of my life as I continue to seek You and depend on You. I will never be the same again. In Jesus' name, I pray. Amen.

If you said this prayer and sincerely meant it, congratulations! Heaven's angels are rejoicing with you (Luke 15:10). The Father, Son, and Holy Spirit are celebrating and throwing a party just for you. Welcome into the family of God's kingdom!

If you prayed this prayer for the first time, please contact me at www.nicholemarbach.com. I would like to personally welcome you into God's family.

ADDENDUM

THE BIRTH OF A MINISTRY

Never in my life did I set out to have a ministry or be a writer. For many years, my sole focus was on surviving. I just wanted to live! During my time of sickness and depression, I never once thought to myself, *This is going to make a great testimony someday.* That thought didn't cross my mind because I didn't believe I would ever be healed.

It wasn't until after I was healed and set free that people started asking me to share my testimony. The first time I spoke about my healing was after only a couple of months of realizing that I was truly free, but the passion in my voice was obvious to everyone who heard me. People could hear and see that the Lord had set me free from past bondages. After that opportunity, God continued to open more doors for me to tell of all He had done in my life.

One of the greatest things that happened after my healing was hearing God's voice. I knew that He had always been speaking to my spirit, as He does to all of His children, but now I was able to hear Him clearly. It was such a relief to hear His voice instead of those of torment. The Father knew I had a deficit of positive, loving, life-giving words in my life, so He began depositing them into my spirit so I could continue to walk in healing and grow in His knowledge.

I started writing in a journal the words He spoke to me and even began receiving prophetic words for Lisa and Anita. Lisa told me that she and Anita believed I had the gift of prophecy. *Wow! I had a gift!* Amazed, I continued to write the words God gave me to encourage others.

After doing this for a while, I sent prophetic words to a ministry that distributes prophecies around the world. I submitted some of the words the Lord gave me, and they accepted every one. Afterward, I received feedback from people telling me how the words touched their lives. I thought of how I went from a person that no one would listen to because I was seen as crazy, to being a voice of encouragement from the Lord.

It wasn't long after I began sending these words out that God said to me, "I want you to write a devotional book." Then, I received the following word from the Lord as a confirmation:

"Daughter, I want you to start using your hands. For I have given you the power to write, and … I'm even going to cause you to begin to write. You can call it poetry, you can call it love notes, you can call it whatever, but I have given you the power to write, daughter. I want you to start writing down things that I will place in your spirit.

"Daughter, I want you to begin to write things down and send them out as letters to people who are hurting and going through a hard time. That way, they can open up these letters in their own homes, in the privacy of their own homes, and they will begin to read. That way, My Spirit can come in when it's just them and Me, and My Spirit will begin to draw them closer and let them understand how much I love them.

"I have given you a writing ability, and I want you to begin to execute. I want you to begin to carry out that command of writing, not just for Me, daughter, but for My people as well. Yes, you have been in a place in your life where you have been rejected, and you know what it's like to be rejected. Even though I never ordained for you to walk through rejection, through that rejection and through that test, I will build a great testimony."

I published my first book in 2011 and have since written three other books, one of which has been translated into Spanish. During my bondage and struggles, when I was considered mentally ill, no one listened to anything I had to say. God Has completely turned that around, and today I speak about His love and encouragement to many people all over the world through books, an online ministry, and speaking engagements. This absolutely amazes me!

I'm invited to share my testimony at meetings, conferences, and recovery groups in order to give people hope and spread God's love and the truth of His Word. I have ministered throughout the United States, Mexico, and Thailand, and have been invited to speak in South Africa. But, I believe the best is yet to come.

I'm so grateful for the healing power of God in my life. I could never do any of this in my own strength. It's His supernatural power flowing through me that makes it possible. This same power is available to everyone. God is truly the God of restoration! He can take someone like me, who was mentally ill and suicidal, to a place of being a voice for His goodness.

I never dreamed that I would be ministering to so many people in so many places, but I wouldn't have it any other way. I never

ever get tired of sharing my testimony and teaching and speaking about God's love and grace. The Lord put me back on His path and led me right to the center of His will for my life.

LOVE LETTERS

Not only did God call me to write in order to bless others, but He used my writing as part of my own healing journey. He "downloaded" numerous love letters to me that I compiled into my book, *Love Notes to My Beloved* (please see Resources from Nichole Marbach Ministries for information on all of my books).

Below is a sampling of these "love letters." Please receive them as if they were written directly to you from your Father God. And, these aren't only for women. Men, simply replace "daughter" with "son," and know that God is speaking to you as well. Allow these words to soak deep into your soul, and receive the overwhelming love that your Daddy has for you.

Day 3 — The Key to Perfect Peace

"My beloved, I want to share with you the key to perfect peace in your life. In Isaiah 26:3, I said, 'You will keep him in perfect peace, whose mind is stayed on you: because he trusts in you' (KJV). I created My children with minds, and I know that sometimes it is hard to get rid of negative, distracting thoughts and not think as the world thinks, but I want to remind you that you are not of this world. You were transferred into another kingdom, another place altogether. When you focus on what I say about you, the incredible inheritance you have in Christ through the Holy Spirit, who lives in you, and focus on Me and listen for My voice speaking to you

and guiding you, I guarantee you that you will be filled with perfect peace. This will be a noticeable peace that those around you will observe as well. It will transform your life. Your life goes in the direction of your dominant thoughts, precious one. My Word says that to be carnally minded is death but to be spiritually minded is life and peace (Romans 8:6). Beloved, have grace on yourself in the process of transforming your mind and thoughts. You will get there. I will help you because I love you so much, and I want to see you walking in My perfect peace."

Declaration of the day:

"I can walk in perfect peace no matter what by keeping my focus on Jesus. He is my perfect peace. When my mind starts to think negatively, I will remind myself to think spiritually minded instead. Peace is mine!"

Day 6 — You Are Not a Failure!

"Beloved, you are not a failure! Don't ever listen to any accusing voices calling you a failure. You may have made some mistakes, but you are not a mistake! You are not a failure. Beloved, I know you get discouraged sometimes when you see a promise in My Word that is not coming to pass in your life. I don't want you to get into discouragement or condemnation, thinking that you are a failure and that is the reason it is not coming to pass in your life. That's a lie. I am a giver, not a withholder. Seek Me on the lie you are believing that is preventing you from receiving what is rightfully yours. I want to help you in this, My daughter. I love you and want to see all of the promises that are yours manifesting in your life. I want you to see yourself as an overcomer, not a failure. I want you to see yourself as victorious, not a victim. I want you to see yourself with resurrection power flowing out of you, not a powerless person. You have

My power in you. I want you to see yourself the way that I see you, and sometimes that is a process of renewing your mind, precious one. Don't give up. Seek Me for more revelation through My Word of who you are in Me and what you have. Proclaim the promises over you. Declare that they are yours! This will help you to believe and receive all the promises in the Word that belong to you, My beloved."

Declaration of the day:

"I am not giving up on the promises that are mine in Christ. My Daddy is going to help me with this. He is going to show me any lies I am believing to lead me to the victory that is already mine!"

Day 44— There Is Nothing Wrong with You, Beloved

"Beloved, when you feel as if you have been rejected by people, and you start to hear those voices telling you, 'There is something wrong with me. People reject me because I am unlovable.' Or, 'I will never be accepted,' I want you to stop and immediately put your focus on Me. Those voices are lies. They come from the enemy who is called the accuser. The enemy wants you to feel rejected and alone and feel like there is something wrong with you because he constantly wants you to feel condemned and unworthy. Those are lies. The truth is that you will always be accepted, loved, and safe with Me. You can never be separated from true love in Me. I want you to focus on Me and how much I love and accept you. I want you to focus on who you are in Me. In Me, you are worthy. In Me, you are loved; passionately loved. If you focus on My love for you, insecurity will leave. If you focus on people rejecting you and the lies that come with it, you will start to feel depressed. Beloved, I want you to stay focused on the truth and ignore those lies when they come your way. The truth is that you are loved, accepted,

worthy, blameless, more than a conqueror, and victorious in Me. You are not a victim in Me. You could not be loved any more than you are loved right now, precious one. There is nothing wrong with you. I see everything right with you because I view you through the blood of My Son and in your spirit!"

Declaration of the day:

"There is nothing wrong with me! I am loved and accepted. I am not a victim. I choose to focus on the truth, not lies. I am loved!"

THE HOPE CENTER

Several years ago, Claude had a dream where he saw me ministering in an office space. That dream blessed me because it had always been my desire to teach and minister to people in a group setting. Over the years, I never forgot about that dream. I believed that sometime in the future it would become reality.

About five years after my husband's dream, I began leading a women's monthly ministry meeting in my basement. It wasn't long before the crowd outgrew my basement, and I knew it was time to look for a larger place for Nichole Marbach Ministries.

While searching for the perfect space, a few places that had looked very promising fell through unexpectedly. I had even signed a contract to share a 5,000-square-foot area with friends of mine who pastored a church, but it also fell through. I then decided to stop looking for a while until I felt the Lord prompt me again, letting me know the timing was right.

I called a realtor friend, and we started searching for a space for my ministry.

At first, we focused on finding a place to rent, but that went nowhere. I was initially disappointed, but then God gave us the idea to invest through purchasing.

The first spaces we sought after were about 2,500 square feet, as I wanted to host small conferences and other small-scale events in an area that size. We placed an offer on a building near my home, which I thought would be perfect. The offer was declined, as the owner decided to increase the asking price by a substantial amount at the last minute. Again, I was disappointed that nothing was working out.

The next day, the Lord led me to search online for office spaces in Bolingbrook, Illinois. Through this search, I found a large condo unit for sale in a retail center with other businesses around it. The realtor and I went to see it and were shocked by what a disaster it was on the inside! The remnants of this former school were apparent, as children's drawings covered the floor, random pieces of furniture lay strewn about, and electric cords dangled from severely damaged ceiling tiles.

Yet, even among the mess, I envisioned this space completely beautiful and perfect for Nichole Marbach Ministries. On top of that, the 5,000-square-foot structure was far less expensive than the 2,500-square-foot space on which I had previously made an offer. After a long process of negotiations and nearly giving up on reaching a deal, we finally arrived at the point of being ready to close on the property.

I had allowed God many opportunities to close this door, but He kept solving every challenge that came our way. In fact, one day when I was feeling overwhelmed and experiencing doubt about continuing on with the sale, the Father had me look on the floor of the lobby. He highlighted one particular school drawing that I had never noticed, although it had been there the whole time. As soon as it caught my eye, joy and peace flooded my heart.

A boy named Kevin had drawn a heart and a cross, then drew a line encircling both. I couldn't believe my eyes. Kevin's drawing was the same basic image that I had been using as a logo for Nichole Marbach Ministries for years! This drawing, that had lay on the floor for possibly several years while the school remained vacant, was prepared by our good God to be there in advance so I'd see it the day I felt apprehensive about purchasing the space. He used it as a confirmation that this was where He wanted me.

Kevin's Drawing

Nichole Marbach Ministries Logo

I'll never forget what God did for me in that moment, as I had to bring it to my remembrance many times to help me navigate through the obstacles of securing our new location. The week before our closing, we were hit with some bad news: The pin number associated with the property included an additional 2,000 square feet of office space that was attached to our property. Another business had been renting this space, but it was owned by the same owner who was selling to us.

We discovered that it could take up to six months to fix the pin number. At that point, I had enough and was ready to walk away. Claude, however, had the idea to negotiate at an extraordinarily low price for the extra space. The owner didn't want to lose the sale, so he reluctantly agreed to Claude's offer. Due to God's favor, we were able to purchase a 7,000-square-foot location at an incredible price.

We immediately got to work, completely renovating the former school and making it look brand new. I decided to name it The HOPE Center, which I believe was rather prophetic, since the inside was once a mess but then became a brand-new creation! The Father told me that He will send me those who feel hope-less—like a total mess on the inside—to The HOPE Center. When they leave, they will know that they have become a new creation in Christ.

The HOPE Center is the home of grace-based conferences, sem-inars, recovery groups, comedy nights (laughter is medicine), Grace Immersion Meetings, Charis Bible studies (affiliated with Charis Bible College), and so much more. I'd also like to one day in the near future add week-long intensive schools, where those who are struggling to overcome mental illness and addictions can renew their minds to the Word of God, listen to powerful healing testimonies, share their hearts in a safe place, and receive one-on-one prayer ministry.

I envision people leaving The HOPE Center with more than hope, although hope in itself is powerful. But, I also see them leaving with true victory in Christ. The HOPE Center is a safe place where people will find hope, healing, and wholeness in Jesus. It's a place with no condemnation, regardless of where people are in their journeys. My vision for the HOPE Center is still unfolding, and it is definitely beyond me. It's a huge vision that only the Father can fulfill—financially, and in every other way.

I want to encourage you that if you have a dream in your heart, as I did, don't give up on it! Our dreams may take time to fulfill, depending on God's timing, but keep trusting your heavenly Father. He will fulfill those dreams that He's given you beyond what you could ever imagine or think possible (Ephesians 3:20). He is the God of abundance! He does things over the top, in a good way.

Keep that dream in your heart, and allow your Father speak to you about it. He'll lead you and guide you until your dream has manifested, and then you can both celebrate it together. He's faithful to do what He has promised.

A SPECIAL THANKS TO THOSE WHO WALKED WITH ME

God has brought me a long way since my initial healing. One thing I've learned through my experiences is that God uses people in the body of Christ during our healing journeys. If you need help, please don't hesitate to get it. Help is available. God didn't call us to walk through our struggles alone.

I thank God for those whom He puts in our paths that can help us understand more deeply who we are in Christ. They can open our eyes to discover the lies that we're believing, which we may not even realize are affecting us. God will send us people who, through the power of the Holy Spirit, can lead us to the healing and wholeness that Jesus paid the price for us to freely obtain.

Personally, God has used many people throughout my journey at different times, such as my husband, my high school track coach, pastors, mentors, Christian counselors, numerous friends, healing ministers, spiritual "parents," and teachers. I am forever grateful for how God used these people in my life.

God used my husband, Claude, at every stage of my journey. Claude has been instrumental in demonstrating to me the unconditional love of Christ. I gave him every reason in the world to leave me, but he never left. He continued to love me, no matter how bad our lives became.

I'm eternally thankful that he stuck by my side, and I look forward to the day that he writes his side of our story to help others like himself, who find themselves caring for someone like me. We both enjoy sharing our story to give others hope. Together, we're raising our three beautiful children, and our family has been restored and healed. I love my husband and am so grateful that when I prayed for a husband as a little girl, God knew He would one day bring Claude into my life from the other side of the world.

God also worked through my track coach in high school to show me a father figure that I never had. What a blessing it was to receive some form of love from a "father"! He spoke life and encouragement to me when I needed it most. Who knows if I would've made it had he not spoken words of life to me before I began to fall apart? He'll always have a special place in my heart.

During my years of bondage, God used my pastor, Fred, and his wife, Ingrid, to walk alongside me and show me the love of Christ. They never gave up on me and were always available when I needed them. During this time, my church family was integral in blessing my family with meals and babysitting and anything else we needed. I'm certain we wouldn't have made it through this time without them in our lives. God used my pastors and our church throughout the bad times, and I'll never forget all that they've done for me.

Additionally, God used Lisa tremendously when I was first healed to mentor me in His love and grace and to keep me in the truths of His Word so I could remain free. She recommended books to me and encouraged me in my identity in Christ. I am thankful to God for placing her in my life during the beginning of my healing journey.

God also put a wonderful Christian counselor/life coach across my path who understands the finished work of Christ. Melanie provided the nurturing, mother figure that I never had, and she became a critical part of my emotional healing. She's a solid, loving, consistent presence who's helped me rebuild trust in relationships. To this day, she encourages and supports me with wisdom that has helped not only in my healing journey but also in the ministry call on my life. I'm grateful to have her as a spiritual mom in my life.

God gave me another great friend in Kimm Oostman, who loved me unconditionally and made me laugh when I desperately needed to during my sicknesses. She was a friend who always encouraged and uplifted me in my times of self-destruction. She believed in me and supported me through the good and the bad. I thank the Lord for sending Kimm my way.

I'm also appreciative for all the other amazing friends who are currently in my life. God uses them to encourage me, to make me laugh, to give me wisdom, and to have fun with. I love to encourage them as well.

A major catalyst to my spiritual development that God brought across my path was Charis Bible College, founded by Andrew

Wommack. About six years after my healing, I began attending CBC. What I learned there was instrumental in helping me renew my mind to my identity in Christ and provide me with a solid biblical foundation. The spiritual growth I gained at CBC exponentially increased my healing. I enrolled in Charis' three-year program and was saturated in the Word of God for hours and hours through various speakers and DVDs. The three-year program is said to be equivalent to being in church for about twenty-five years!

The knowledge of God's love and grace that I received at Charis caused me to be a better wife, a better mother, and a better person. It helped me to effortlessly change into the woman I was created to be and to fall deeper in love with Jesus.

It's not an exaggeration to say that Andrew Wommack Ministries and Charis Bible College changed my life. I reached out to the ministry regarding my testimony when I was a student at CBC, sharing with them that I believed there needed to be more mental illness and addiction healing testimonies reported. They agreed with me, and eventually filmed my story to use as part of their *Healing Journey* DVD series. They have since included my testimony on the Andrew Wommack Ministry website as well, in order to share hope and healing with others.

Charis focuses on the love and grace of God—the good news of the gospel. There are satellite locations all over the world, as well as online and correspondence options for those wanting to study from home. I highly recommend Charis for its immersion in God's Word and the fellowship with other like-minded believers provided on its campuses. (Please see Recommended Ministries and Resources at the end of this book for contact information on Charis Bible College and Andrew Wommack Ministries.)

We're all a part of God's kingdom family. We *are* family. God knew that we'd need each other. He didn't create us to isolate ourselves from one another. He created us to be in relationship with Him and with the body of Christ. I'll always be thankful to God for the amazing people He's placed in my life. I wouldn't be who I am today without their influence. Honestly, I don't think I'd even be alive today if I didn't have His support system during my darkest days.

If you feel isolated and alone, ask the Father to place His trusted people in your path, and He'll do it. He may ask you to take a step of faith and meet new people. Other people don't always just magically appear in our lives. We usually need to make some effort to meet them.

If you have a fear of rejection as I did, pray against that, and remind yourself how loved you are by Father God. Ask the Lord to give you the courage to step out in faith and find others to fellowship with. That's a godly desire, and God loves to give us the desires of our heart (Psalm 37:4).

The following is a prayer to get you started:

Heavenly Father, I feel isolated. I have a desire for more fellowship. I pray that You would help me to find trusted people to be a part of my life. I ask You for wisdom to know how to find these people. I know that You'll lead and guide me in this. I also ask that You would give me the courage to take a step of faith to try to make new friends. Father, show me who You have in mind for me. I know You want to connect me with the right people, and I believe that You will. I look forward to this new adventure with You and others. In Jesus' name, amen.

WITNESS ACCOUNTS OF HEALING

Some people reading my story may doubt the extent of my trauma and bondage before I was healed or the miraculous healing that ultimately ensued in my life. I've included this chapter in my book as a testimony to the truth of my journey. The following accounts of my healing were written by a leader of a Christian recovery group I had participated in and three very dear friends who were with me throughout the deepest and darkest valleys of my mental illness and addictions. These friends were beside me every step of the way, encouraging me, loving me, and speaking the truth to me in love, but also being frustrated and hopeless with not knowing how to help me. They stuck by me through it all, and I am forever grateful for them.

All of these people were willing to share a small piece of my journey from their perspective in order for others to understand how good God is and how He truly is the God of the impossible. Like me, they want others to know that there's absolutely no one who is beyond hope in God's eyes.

It's impossible to put all of the details of my story into the pages of this book, but I believe my words will help others see what life was like for me and for those around me.

The other day someone asked me about healing. My response was to tell them the story of my friend Nichole and how I have watched her become transformed and free. The Nichole I met many years ago was a woman who was only happy when she was in pain or intoxicated. The physical pain she brought on herself was easier than the emotional pain that she couldn't deal with.

When I'd try to care for her, she'd push me away, only to come back begging for a relationship with me. My husband, Fred, once told her, in her lowest moment, that one day she would hold her head up high. She did not believe him.

I have taken Nichole to the emergency room after failed suicide attempts, visited her in locked psychiatric wards, and sat with her in psychiatric offices, as her multiple diagnoses were explained to her husband. There were many times when it was impossible to befriend Nichole, and there were few ways to show her love. But, my friend is not that woman anymore. She has been completely healed. My husband and I bear testimony to this. God has turned her mourning into dancing. Her tears are now laughter. It warms my heart to hear her talk about her love of laughing, when all I can remember is her tears and pain. The power of the risen Christ has transformed Nichole's life, just as it has transformed my own — and can transform yours as well.

Ingrid D.
Plainfield, Illinois, USA

"Do you think someone is an alcoholic if they drink every week?" Nichole asked me one day. Her question should've triggered something in me. It was a strange question to ask since she didn't know me very well. But Nichole and I worked together like bread and butter, as if we had known each other for a long time. I immediately started processing her question logically, which she probably counted on happening. I liked having a friend who'd call me wanting to talk; she liked having a friend who assured her she was "normal."

But, what was really going on with her question? Nichole was looking for a way to explain away or justify things happening in her life that she knew weren't right. At the beginning of our friendship, she was already lying and sneaking alcohol to numb her pain. I don't think she was ever convinced that there was anything wrong with it and maybe didn't even know why she was compelled to do such things. But it soon became a pattern.

Every time she was faced with a new challenge, a new diagnosis, or a new label, Nichole went on a fact-finding mission in an attempt to disprove what people were telling her, all the while spinning out of control. She had me convinced that she could manage her life, and I tried to reassure her that she was doing just fine.

I still remember one particular conversation with Nichole and her husband, Claude: "We're updating our paperwork and are wondering if you and Ken will be guardians to our kids if something were to ever happen to us." Their request made perfect sense, as our three children and their three children were all close in age and played together all the time. We were both stay-at-home moms and would exchange childcare or get together just to talk about life. We'd talk about lessons learned in her counseling *and commiserate about our rough childhoods. I knew that watching her kids or having mine play at her house was what she needed to help her keep everyone busy so she could just get through the day.*

As the years rolled by and Nichole went from one doctor to the next, trying to figure out how to function, trying with counselors to untangle the spider web of pain woven during childhood, trying to regulate her many medications, and trying to be a wife and mother, it was clear that things weren't really getting better.

Sometimes I really envied Nichole's life: She had a husband who adored and doted on her, three beautiful children, a wonderful home in a very desirable neighborhood, financial stability, and European vacations. I didn't see myself as being in that same position. But, for Nichole, I could see how it made her feel, knowing that she had all that, yet she still couldn't function and wanted to end her life. It was a tremendous catalyst for shame.

Sometimes I'd go to Nichole's house, and she could barely make eye contact or participate in conversation. I really don't think any of us understood the enormous battle being waged over her thoughts, her spirit, and quite literally, her life. To her credit, through trying to be transparent and accountable, others came to learn of her struggles. I remember one truly concerned friend at church asking, "How is Nichole really doing?" Sadly, and I can't believe I said this out loud, but with a broken and worried heart, I replied, "I wouldn't be surprised if Claude calls me one day and says she's gone." By "gone," I meant dead. It was that bad, and I knew she was that low. None of us knew how to help anymore.

One day I was lying on the couch with the flu. Nichole called and begged me to come over. Sometimes it was exhausting being her friend, yet she always made me feel needed and authentically loved. But this time I said no. She begged me again. "No. I have the flu," I persisted. "I have a fever. You wouldn't want me there. I can't come!" That was the day she ended up in the emergency room after Claude came home and found her covered in blood. The next day, I went to her house to talk with Claude. Like me, he was exhausted, but also deeply saddened. I've never seen in a man's eyes the amount of sadness he was experiencing. He was broken. Through counselors, doctors, prayers, and support, nothing had made a difference. Where did we go from here to help Nichole get better? We all wanted to know.

As painful as it was, I think all of those ups and downs, the diagnoses, medications, rehabs, recovery groups, and counselors were all part of a larger plan. The turning point came when Nichole joined a recovery group that taught her—along with all of us—that this was spiritual darkness at work. From what I thought was an incurable disease, bipolar disorder, we were reminded that Christ can heal. Know that—Christ can heal us! We were so caught up in the world of "knowable" answers and medicine fixes that we forgot, or didn't understand, the overarching miracle of Christ!

I know there are various plans and paths for everyone. Christ's work in each of our lives will look very different. However, I can truly say I know someone who received healing from an "incurable" disease. Nichole's healing and shedding of her labels and what she has transformed into, by the sweet mercy of Jesus, has changed lives. Rather than staying silent about all of her truths, as embarrassing and shameful as people might consider them to be, she uses her story to help others.

Nichole knows firsthand that to "die is gain" and to "live is Christ" (Philippians 1:21). She has shown this by humbly allowing God to complete His work in her life. She gives back to her family, community, and *fellowship through Nichole Marbach Ministries. By providing worship experiences, healing prayer, free resources to those in need, and always listening to God's call for her next steps, she works for Him.*

Our days as young mothers, trying to figure out how to raise young children under the expectations of suburbia and Christian perfection, are long gone. Our children have grown up, and our families live far away from one another. Yet, we will forever share our experience of enduring, selfless, and authentic friendship, born of Christ's steadfast love for us both.

Kimm O.
Albuquerque, New Mexico

◆•••◆•••◆•••◆•••◆•••◆•••◆

When Nichole first revealed to me how much she was drinking, I was completely shocked. I had no idea that alcohol was an issue for her because as far as I could see, she functioned normally. As I got to know her, I learned that we had a lot in common, and we could really make each other laugh. I had no idea there was such pain behind her smile. She also started sharing how deeply some of her pain and anxiety was rooted.

Nichole's unrest was evident, and she always appeared nervous. She continually bounced her knee when she sat, and she kept herself quite busy. I was amazed and a little jealous of her constant energy! In fact, the walls in her house changed color regularly because she was always painting them. I think she felt that if she just kept moving, she could make it through that minute, then the hour, and then the day.

For years, Nichole was diagnosed with a different mental health label on a regular basis and tried doctors, counselors, treatment programs, and many varieties of medications to help her keep her head above water. I know she often thought of suicide, and I was really afraid I was going to lose her. It didn't seem as if anything was working. As a friend, I felt desperate to help her but with no idea how.

I remember driving down the road after having a difficult and frustrating day with Nichole, and the song "Neither Will I" by Twila Paris came on my iPod. "He will never give up on you, and neither will I," Twila sang. I cried and prayed for strength to never give up on Nichole and for her to never give up on herself or Jesus. I prayed for her husband and kids who were also frustrated and worn out.

After years of agony, Nichole became a part of a recovery group that taught her that instead of fighting the varying diagnoses, to fight the real enemy behind her problems—Satan. As she'd talk about spiritual warfare, I listened with wide eyes and heard things that I had never learned in church. She was getting better, and it really opened my heart to miracle healing. I'm not sure why I was so shocked by Nichole's complete healing. I've read about Jesus' miracles in the Bible, but seeing it with my own two eyes is something very different. I'll never be the same. I have often used Nichole's story to encourage others.

Now, instead of hiding in the shame of the past, Nichole is bravely putting her story out there to help others learn the love and healing power of Jesus! You go, my friend!

Kim B.
Pella, Iowa

I was the senior woman's group leader in my church's healing and recovery ministry for over four years when God brought Nichole to our ministry, and then into my small group. I had also been actively leading a deliverance ministry there and was employed as a Clinical Nurse Specialist in Psychiatry for twenty-four years.

Outside of a locked, inpatient psychiatric unit, I had never closely encountered someone so broken as Nichole. She never made eye contact, always looked down, and said she only felt safe with me because I could understand all of her diagnoses and labels.

She had no confidence when speaking in the small group or even on the phone. She only felt safe to express her deep thoughts and feelings to me, which she often did several times a day, in lengthy and detailed emails. Dark, entangled lies were evident in her thoughts and emotions, which were most often reflected in thoughts of harming herself.

The Holy Spirit gave me His responses to her emails time and time and time again. She was taking hold of those truths here and there but was also being strongly tempted to resort to the self-destructive patterns that had been so deeply rooted and established in her for years.

The enemy also tempted me with fearful thoughts, making me believe that her most recent email to me would be the final one. He tempted me to believe that she would be found dead, and I'd be held responsible for trying to help her through emails, when I should've called the police and had her committed to a psychiatric ward.

The Holy Spirit strengthened and encouraged us both in different ways. My small group co-leader, Lisa, knew of my heavy heart and prayed for me, as well as Nichole, and our journey together.

What an awesome joy to have witnessed God's healing grace—believed, received, and walked out by Nichole over these years. I too was transformed by the Holy Spirit to witness and be a part of what He was doing in her, as I was better able to believe for others who were in deep bondage as Nichole was.

Anita P.
Mooresville, NC

PHOTOGRAPHS
AND RESOURCES

PHOTOGRAPHS OF MEDICAL DIAGNOSES

BEHAVIORAL HEALTH SERVICES
ADULT PROGRESS NOTES

Name: Nichole Marbach Age: 33 Medical Record Number: 1066880 Account:

Attending Physician: ▓▓▓▓▓▓▓ M.D. Assigned Clinician: ▓▓▓▓▓ LCPC, CADC

Date: ▓▓▓▓ Time: 9am-4pm Program: PHP

_x_ Individual ___ Group ___ Family ___ Marital
_x_ Orientation ___ Psychosocial Assessment
___ Art Therapy ( ) ___ Community
_x_ Expressive Therapy (Draw a card from someone whom you want to hear) _x_ Leisure Education (teambuilding)
___ Patient Education Group ( )
___ Psychodrama ___ Recreational Therapy ( )
_x_ Relaxation Therapy ___ Treatment Plan Review ___ Weekend Planning

Admission Note: Pt. is a 32-year-old Caucasian female who lives with her husband and 3 children ▓▓▓▓▓▓▓▓▓▓▓▓▓
Pt. was referred to BHS's PHP ▓▓▓▓▓ after Pt. slit her wrists last week along with taking an overdose (▓▓▓▓) of Trazadone in
a suicide attempt. This is Pt's 2nd hospital based psychiatric treatment experience; she was admitted inpatient to Hinsdale ▓▓▓▓▓▓▓
and then to their Options PHP program through ▓▓▓▓▓ Pt. was also treated at New Day Program ▓▓ for chemical dependency
issues, primarily alcoholism. Pt. experienced increasing depressive symptoms including hopelessness, irritability and anger outbursts,
anhedonia, tearfulness, self-injury, binge eating, racing thoughts, poor concentration, worsening ability to complete tasks, and poor
sleep. ▓▓▓▓▓▓▓▓▓▓▓▓▓▓▓▓▓▓▓▓▓▓▓▓▓▓▓▓▓ Pt. has a history of self-injury. Pt.
reports passive S/I but is able to contract for safety; she denies H/I. Goals will be to stabilize mood, gain acceptance of bipolar and
borderline diagnoses, reduce/eliminate suicidal ideations, maintain abstinence and relapse prevention, improve healthy self-
soothing/coping techniques, educate on bipolar II mixed episodes and borderline personality disorder, increase support system.
Current medications: Lamictal 100 mg; Trileptal 600 mg; Zoloft 100 mg; Zyprexa 5 mg. Diagnosis: Bipolar II, mixed episodes;
Borderline personality disorder; Alcohol dependence (in remission). Pt. was oriented to program and informed of Pt's rights.

Note: ▓▓▓

Individual session: Pt. presented as shaky, depressed, and anxious. Eye contact was good and she was talkative and cooperative; she
appears motivated for treatment and to feel better. Pt. offered background information regarding family of origin issues including
▓▓▓▓▓▓▓▓▓▓▓▓▓▓▓▓▓▓▓▓▓▓ current situation with husband and her 3 children, her current support network
including AA meetings and aftercare group from Hinsdale, recovery and relapses, anger management issues. Pt. talked about her
shame at having been diagnosed with Bipolar II and Borderline Personality disorders. She intellectually realizes they are illnesses as is
her alcoholism, but is struggling with the stigma that she feels is attached. She feels guilty for not being able to take her 3-year-old son
to daycare this morning on his first day as she did with his sisters. Pt. has several abandonment/rejection issues regarding her family,

Progress Notes, September 2003

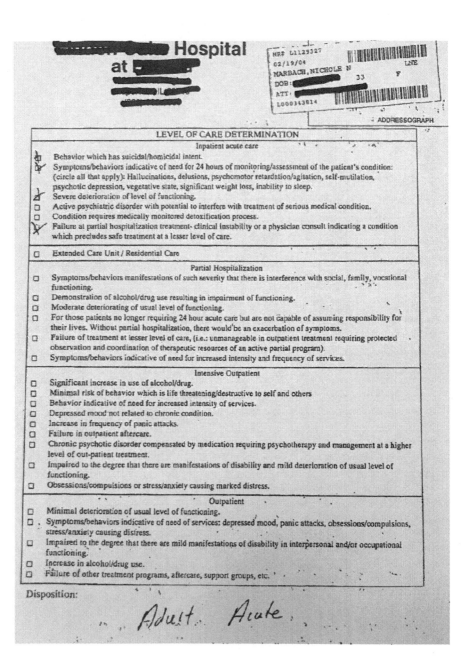

Hospital
at _____

NRF L1123327
02/19/04
MARBACH, NICHOLE N   33   F
DOB:
ATT:
L000343814

ADDRESSOGRAPH

LEVEL OF CARE DETERMINATION

Inpatient acute care

- ☒ Behavior which has suicidal/homicidal intent.
- ☒ Symptoms/behaviors indicative of need for 24 hours of monitoring/assessment of the patient's condition: (circle all that apply): Hallucinations, delusions, psychomotor retardation/agitation, self-mutilation, psychotic depression, vegetative state, significant weight loss, inability to sleep.
- ☒ Severe deterioration of level of functioning.
- ☐ Active psychiatric disorder with potential to interfere with treatment of serious medical condition.
- ☐ Condition requires medically monitored detoxification process.
- ☒ Failure at partial hospitalization treatment- clinical instability or a physician consult indicating a condition which precludes safe treatment at a lesser level of care.

- ☐ Extended Care Unit / Residential Care

Partial Hospitalization

- ☐ Symptoms/behaviors manifestations of such severity that there is interference with social, family, vocational functioning.
- ☐ Demonstration of alcohol/drug use resulting in impairment of functioning.
- ☐ Moderate deteriorating of usual level of functioning.
- ☐ For those patients no longer requiring 24 hour acute care but are not capable of assuming responsibility for their lives. Without partial hospitalization, there would be an exacerbation of symptoms.
- ☐ Failure of treatment at lesser level of care, (i.e.: unmanageable in outpatient treatment requiring protected observation and coordination of therapeutic resources of an active partial program).
- ☐ Symptoms/behaviors indicative of need for increased intensity and frequency of services.

Intensive Outpatient

- ☐ Significant increase in use of alcohol/drug.
- ☐ Minimal risk of behavior which is life threatening/destructive to self and others
- ☐ Behavior indicative of need for increased intensity of services.
- ☐ Depressed mood not related to chronic condition.
- ☐ Increase in frequency of panic attacks.
- ☐ Failure in outpatient aftercare.
- ☐ Chronic psychotic disorder compensated by medication requiring psychotherapy and management at a higher level of out-patient treatment.
- ☐ Impaired to the degree that there are manifestations of disability and mild deterioration of usual level of functioning.
- ☐ Obsessions/compulsions or stress/anxiety causing marked distress.

Outpatient

- ☐ Minimal deterioration of usual level of functioning.
- ☐ Symptoms/behaviors indicative of need of services: depressed mood, panic attacks, obsessions/compulsions, stress/anxiety causing distress.
- ☐ Impaired to the degree that there are mild manifestations of disability in interpersonal and/or occupational functioning.
- ☐ Increase in alcohol/drug use.
- ☐ Failure of other treatment programs, aftercare, support groups, etc.

Disposition:

Adult. Acute.

Hospital Diagnosis, February 2004

LINDEN OAKS HOSPITAL
NAPERVILLE, ILLINOIS   L1129327

PATIENT NAME: MARBACH, NICOLE
ACCOUNT #: 000343814

DISCHARGE SUMMARY

Unit - Adult inpatient psychiatry, Linden Oaks Hospital

DISCHARGE DIAGNOSES:
AXIS I: Bipolar II disorder, impulse control disorder, not
           otherwise specified. Alcohol abuse.
AXIS II: Borderline personality disorder.
AXIS III: No apparent acute.
AXIS IV: Moderate social stressors.
AXIS V: 35.

HISTORY OF PRESENT ILLNESS:
The patient is a 33-year-old married Caucasian female who
presented to the hospital after having worsening suicidal
ideation. The patient attempted to kill herself by overdosing on
her medications and cutting her wrist. The patient reports that
she had been in therapy over the past two years, however, over
the past two weeks became increasingly depressed and became
acutely suicidal. The patient also relapsed on alcohol for the
past two weeks and such has contributed to her worsening guilt.
The patient reports positive insomnia, anhedonia, crying spells,
chronic suicidal ideation, and also significant self-mutilation.
The patient notes vague past manic episodes with increased
energy and decreased sleep, irritable moods, and racing thoughts.
The patient denies past psychotic symptoms. The patient denied
substance use other than alcohol, however, urine toxicology is
positive for PCP and amphetamines. Attempt to get confirmatory
test was unsuccessful.

Discharge Report, February 2004

2. Patient is suffering from an incapacitating anxiety/panic episode requiring PHP to stabilize, as evidenced by :		6.	Patient suffering from incapacitating thought problems requiring PHP to stabilize, as evidenced by:
3. Patient is suffering from an incapacitating manic-hypomanic episode requiring PHP to stabilize, as evidenced by: anxiety attacks, racing thoughts, high level of irritability, mood swings and outbursts of anger.		7.	Patient also suffering from incapacitating alcohol and drug use, as evidenced by daily, increasing use of alcohol during IOP and misuse of Ativan, history of binge drinking, patient reported drinking alcohol each treatment day at lunch, she has history of previous alcohol

Hospital Diagnosis, October 2005

Discharge Report, November 2005

PHOTOGRAPHS OF
THE HOPE CENTER

Lobby Area

Main Conference Room

Main Conference Room

Café 22 Counter

Café 22 Seating Area

RECOMMENDED MINISTRIES AND RESOURCES

The following ministries and resources have had a tremendous impact on my life. If you desire to grow in the love and grace of God, I highly recommend the following:

Andrew Wommack Ministries

Founder, Andrew Wommack

www.awmi.net

Andrew Wommack Ministries provides free podcasts and articles on its website. Subjects include healing, righteousness, authority, hope, and much more.

Recommended books from Andrew Wommack Ministries:

God Wants You Well
Grace—The Power of the Gospel
The Believer's Authority
The War Is Over!
You've Already Got It!

Charis Bible College
Founder, Andrew Wommack

www.charisbiblecollege.org

Charis Bible College is an international non-accredited college focused on teaching directly from God's Word about His unconditional love and grace. Headquartered in beautiful Woodland Park, Colorado, CBC has satellite campuses around the world. CBC offers two- or three-year and on-site, as well as online and correspondence programs.

Freedom Living Ministries
Founder, Sandra McCollom

www.sandramccollom.com

Sandra is a great friend who's passionate about seeing people set free with the gospel of grace. I encourage you to visit her website and blog to be uplifted with God's good news.

Recommended book from Sandra McCollom:

I Tried Until I Almost Died —
From Anxiety & Frustration to Rest & Relaxation

Joseph Prince Ministries

Founder, Joseph Prince

www.josephprince.org

Joseph Prince has a life-changing revelation of the Father's love and the finished work of Christ. His many teachings, books, and other resources available for purchase will bring you into a closer walk with the Lord.

Recommended books from Joseph Prince Ministries:

Destined to Reign
Grace Revolution
Unmerited Favor

Parresia Ministries

Founder, Tricia Gunn

www.parresiaministries.com

Tricia is an amazing teacher of the gospel of grace. Her book, Bible studies, and other resources provide growth in the knowledge of Jesus and His finished work on the cross.

Recommended book from Parresia Ministries:

Unveiling Jesus

RESOURCES FROM NICHOLE MARBACH MINISTRIES

Love Letter Devotional Books:

77 Texts from Heaven for Teens
    (XP Publishing, 2012, reprinted 2016 by Createspace)

100 More Love Letters from the Throne of Grace Journal
    (XP Publishing, 2013, reprinted 2016 by Createspace)

122 Love Letters from the Throne of Grace Journal
    (XP Publishing, 2011, reprinted 2016 by Createspace)

Love Notes to My Beloved
    (Createspace, 2015, also available in Spanish)

Teaching and Events:

Ministry teachings are available on the Nichole Marbach Ministries website that will aid in releasing condemnation, help to better understand the love of our good Father, and allow you to receive healing for your heart.

The HOPE Center (home of Nichole Marbach Ministries) in Bolingbrook, Illinois, holds numerous events throughout the year that enable participants to grow in the love and grace of God and discover their true identity in Christ.

Visit **www.nicholemarbach.com** to connect with Nichole and learn more about Nichole Marbach Ministries, upcoming events, and available resources.